INTERIOR VISIONS
Great American Designers and the Showcase House

Chris Casson Madden

Foreword by Mario Buatta

Research Assistance by Jeanne-Marie Casson

Stewart, Tabori & Chang

New York

Published in 1988 by
Stewart, Tabori & Chang, Inc.
740 Broadway, New York, New York 10003

LIBRARY OF CONGRESS CATALOGING-IN-PUBLICATION DATA

Madden, Chris Casson.
    Interior visions : great American designers and the showcase house
  / Chris Casson Madden ; foreword by Mario Buatta.
      p.   cm.
    Includes index.
    ISBN 1-55670-038-5 : $45.00
      1. Interior decoration – United States – History – 20th century.
  2. Interior decorators – United States.   I. Title.
NK2115.M315 1988
728′.0973 – dc19   88-15303
                                                      CIP

Distributed in the U.S. by Workman Publishing,
708 Broadway, New York, New York 10003
Distributed in Canada by Canadian Manda Group,
P.O. Box 920 Station U, Toronto, Ontario M8Z 5P9
Distributed in all other territories by Little,
Brown and Company, International Division, 34 Beacon Street,
Boston, Massachusetts 02108

Printed in Japan

10 9 8 7 6 5 4 3

Page 1: Mark Epstein Designs, Inc.
Page 2: Mary Dial (see also pages 78–79).
Page 3: Clifford Stanton (see also pages 176–177).

CONTENTS

FOREWORD

I was born in an all-white modern house—glass and chrome and steel. I cannot say that I liked it; to me the most unsettling thing in the world is a room that is all white. I remember when I was growing up I loved the lived-in quality of my aunt's house. The walls and tables were covered with possessions that created a private sense of beauty, a scrapbook of her life. A rich variety of decorative objects, stacks of books, photographs, flowers—all spoke of attachments and history. By age eleven I was developing a philosophy about decorating and design—and rearranging my parents' furniture.

It took me a while to find myself in this field, but somehow I always knew I wanted to be a decorator. After studying architecture I began, about twenty-eight years ago, an apprenticeship in the decorating department at B. Altman & Co. I then went to Europe to study under Stanley Barrows in a Parsons School of Design program. It was during this trip that I saw my first real English country houses, and I was intrigued. When I returned to New York I was employed first by Elisabeth Draper, then Keith Irvine, and I ventured out on my own in 1963. Soon after this I took a trip to England, where I met John Fowler of the London firm Colefax and Fowler. He introduced me to the possibilities of combining English design with American know-how, and I became more passionate about and sure of the direction I was taking. Mr. Fowler remains one of the major influences in my professional life.

I love designing voluptuously undecorated rooms, although the need for instant pedigree bothers me a lot. I've been doing my version of the English country look since I began my business and, although I didn't starve in those days, I was nowhere near as successful as I am today. In fact, the English country look is all the rage now. It is flattering to be copied . . . but I know I'll still be approaching design in the same way twenty years from now—only just as current, I hope.

There is no great mystery to design. The real secret is how to make things work, and that is a gift that must be nurtured. Of course, how one designs tells a good deal about oneself. Antiques may speak of mystery or romance; paintings or *objets* may reveal a preoccupation or interest. One would hope that *all* the objects one surrounds oneself with in a room have special meaning. I even fall in love with the pieces I put into my showhouse rooms and find it traumatic to part with them—and the room itself, for that matter—when the house closes.

I credit a great deal of my success to having done showhouses in the late 1960s and early '70s, for it was there that people saw my work and were able to understand what I was all about. I've done more than fourteen showhouses, and I still remember vividly designing my first in 1969, which was done for the benefit of the Vassar Alumni Club of Fairfield County, Connecticut, and participating in the first Kips Bay Boys' Club Decorator Show House, at 70 Street and Park Avenue in New York.

The pressures involved are terrific, especially in terms of time and expense, but what it does for a young designer's career can be incredible. For a showcase house is just that—a showcase of one's work in the best possible situation with the best possible audience coming to see it. It is great exposure, with total freedom and total leeway. Making compromises is a real part of the everyday job, but a showhouse is the one time when people get to see your work as you envision it (as opposed to projects done for clients, when the work is not necessarily a reflection of yourself), and they can judge you on your own taste. Of course, I always want to do what works best in a room—something I can usually feel as soon as I walk into it—but, unfortunately, with showhouses it is sometimes not only a question of what you want to do, but also what you can afford to do.

Doing a room in a showhouse is like giving a party; it is also an art. You make sure that every element of the room is perfection—the furnishings, the fabrics, the lighting, the flowers. The only sad part to me is that instead of being able to enjoy my work forever, as most artists can with a canvas, this room I have created usually lasts only about three weeks and then is taken apart.

To me, the most crucial point about a showhouse room is that it look lived in. These should be rooms that seem to have been there always. Creating these rooms, one has an imaginary client in mind and the idea that the room look as if someone has simply stepped out for a moment. Your eyes are always seeing things that could be different. I rearrange furniture and flowers, light candles, plump pillows, and straighten paintings; changes are inevitable all through the run to keep the room fresh, to make it not static. It is after the showhouse closes that you can judge your success, for it is then that you hear that people have seen the life in the room. And then you know it was perfect.

Mario Buatta

INTRODUCTION

From beginning to end, a showcase house is strangely comparable to a Broadway show. First, it's a limited run—showhouses are open to the public for usually three to six weeks and then dismantled, demolished, or, in some cases, sold intact. Second, the unprecedented flurry of publicity, tickets, and programs calls to mind the behind-the-scenes frenzy of a Broadway production. And, finally, there's even an opening night—usually a black-tie gala.

Walking through a showhouse is an extraordinary design experience. These rooms are not cohesive in the design sense, nor do they try to be. Even a first glimpse lets us know immediately that these spaces are vastly different from any other design form. Each room in a showhouse is a unique and individual environment translated from the dreams of its creator, an interior designer. It is here that the designer can work untrammeled, for these rooms are pure fantasy, created without the restraints of clients or budgets and dependent only on the designer's own creativity, energy, vision, and powers of persuasion.

Varying in size from a jewel box of a town house in New York City to a Hawaiian beachfront home to a fifty-room Georgian estate near Boston, the most successful showhouses are those where the designers are given full creative freedom and are not restricted to a specific theme or color scheme. Showhouses certainly benefit designers' reputations, but they also raise huge sums which are often donated to local hospitals, libraries, medical research organizations, symphony orchestras, scholarship programs, and children's clubs.

The process by which designers are chosen for each of the rooms in a showhouse varies from city to city. Some use a lottery, some draw straws, others have a waiting list, and still others rely on a mysterious method of selection that only a handful of benefit-committee members know. In most cases, however, designers are picked for their excellence in their profession and for their portfolio. And, although a spirit of togetherness develops once the designers and rooms are chosen, there is an edge of competitiveness beforehand, since a reputation can be built on a single room.

Once the list of designers is finally determined, work can officially begin. Measurements are taken, ideas are debated, antiques are begged and borrowed, insurance is purchased, and contractors can be seen removing walls, floors, and ceilings. And while it seems that these rooms are transformed overnight, the metamorphosis usually takes three to eight weeks. In the final forty-eight hours, the tension mounting, heart and soul go into these rooms, as the designers strive for a lived-in yet highly polished look.

Because there are no client demands, the designer can create the room of his or her dreams, using colors and *objets d'art* that are personal favorites. This artistic freedom is enhanced by the astonishing cooperation that the designer receives from the design community. Furniture manufacturers, upholsterers, art galleries, antique dealers, rug and carpet companies, fabric and wallcovering houses—all want to be involved in a showcase house and the tremendous publicity that it spawns, and designers will frequently find themselves the recipients of gracious donations from these firms. Suppliers can be remarkably cooperative about short showhouse deadlines: whereas normal delivery of a chair may take twelve weeks, upholsterers have been known to turn out a pair of chairs over a weekend for a showhouse. It's a winning situation for everyone, and for a designer, access to such superb sources can be an enormous help in creating the ambience that he or she is trying to achieve—and can often provide the perfect finishing touches to a room.

Although showcase houses are feasts of inspiration, they also offer a wealth of practical solutions to everyday design problems. Thus, for the public, showhouses are a rare treat and well worth the price of admission. Not only will showhouse visitors see top-notch designers at work, taking the elements of design and reformulating and recombining them in novel ways, but they'll also see priceless antiques and art objects that span centuries and cultures. They'll witness the latest design trends, for it is here that trompe l'oeil, *faux* and oxidized finishes, historical references, and passementerie were all rediscovered. As guests journey through these different rooms, they'll see myriad unusual window treatments, suggestions for creating more space and improving layouts, the latest design currents, and the newest palette of colors. They'll also have the privilege of viewing architecturally important and, in many cases, historic houses.

Of course, not every room in every showcase house is successful. But in the very best, such as the ones that follow, we see the fresh, the whimsical, the opulent, the prophetic, the unexpected—in short, the best of American interior design.

HALLS

Whether a grand entrance foyer or a cramped vestibule, the hall is one's introduction to a house. The ambience of a hall creates the first impression, often setting the stage for what is about to follow.

Almost all designers of showcase halls and loggias have two major restrictions to contend with. First, their design should reflect the design of the rooms off the hall. Often, however, these rooms are worked on behind closed doors, so the hall designer has no idea of what they look like. A solution for many designers of foyers is to lean toward the conservative or work in the style of the architecture of the room. Second, many of these rooms are oddly shaped or oversized spaces, not the more typical square or rectangular rooms that lend themselves to easy solutions. Some of them, like the 10-by-60-foot Long Island hall that Linda Goodman and Jerry Katz designed, are more like bowling alleys than rooms in a home. These unusual spaces tax the designer's creativity, since general sitting areas and arrangements are much more difficult to map out.

While many of these foyers will have odd architectural details, the designer—through visual tricks such as *faux* finishes and trompe l'oeil—will either completely erase the elements or embellish them, as Marianne von Zastrow did with the niches and columns in one of the halls that follows.

A final practical consideration is that these entryways lead to all the other rooms in the house, which are at various stages of renovation and construction as opening night approaches. Designers, committee members, workers bearing furniture and flowers—all are constantly traipsing through the hall, and most designers find it practical to finish this space at the latest possible date. And since halls are not usually roped off, as some showcase rooms are, the flooring must be incredibly durable to withstand the beating that thousands of feet will inflict. For example, besides the fact that the Louis XIII–style Savonnerie rug was perfect for the large hall that McMillen designed for the Kips Bay showhouse, the designers knew that this antique rug could take the wear and tear of visitor traffic, unlike a chenille or a delicate needlepoint. But whatever the floor or walls or window treatment, each of these halls reflects its designer's passionate determination to create a memorable space.

*The entrance hall of the Clayton Mark
House, designed by David O'Neill in 1987.*

12

Unusual for New England, the original inspiration for the Colonial Revival–style Lyman estate *(above)* was Dutch rather than English. This prompted designer Jane Viator to incorporate Continental touches such as the thread-lace window treatment and the *faux-lapis* column topped by a flower arrangement that was copied from a Flemish still life. "Practicality, economy, and respect for the past suggested the emphasis on painted finishes as the major decorative strategy," explains the designer. This fresh and welcoming atmosphere was produced through a combination of paint and imagination. Ragged-and-sponged upper walls, marbleized dado, and trompe l'oeil "tile" floor recall the gracious prewar era when the house was built: a period of meticulous craftsmanship and informed interest in historic styles.

The round *faux-bois* boxes rest unobtrusively on a shelf, underscoring a nineteenth-century Flemish landscape print by Koehler that gives the impression of being held up by trompe l'oeil ribbon.

The grand entrance foyer *(opposite)* in the Kirkeby estate in Bel Air, California, was reinterpreted by Kalef Aleton and Craig Wright as a tribute to the distinguished late designer Michael Taylor. The house, considered by the cognoscenti to be the finest reproduction of eighteenth-century French Neoclassical architecture in Los Angeles, was built in the 1930s. The marble-lined foyer is lighted with a Waterford chandelier, 10 feet in diameter, which hangs over an important Louis XV parcel-gilt console table from the Rothschild collection. An exceptional grouping of seventeenth-century mother-of-pearl is displayed amongst orchids and candles, while four Venetian blackamoors flank the main doors, which lead into the drawing room.

Gail Leddy's skilled use of perspective in this hallway conjures up a succession of rooms, inspired by the painting *View Down a Corridor,* by the Dutch artist Samuel van Hoogstraten. Aside from the mirror, chandelier, and sconces, this 18-by-9-foot mural is entirely trompe l'oeil, including the limestone walls. Executed in canvas by Simonson & Baric, it was hung like wallpaper in three pieces—to keep the heavy mural from falling—and then painted. Because of the narrowness of the landing, it is possible to get the full effect of the mural only from the staircase.

14

16

Marianne von Zastrow's talent as a painter can be seen when one realizes that the archway, overdoor, and two columns on either side of the gated opening are trompe l'oeil. She created these elements to complement the two existing, now *faux-marbre*, columns. The large niche seen on the left is real; the smaller one next to it is trompe l'oeil. On the right wall, where bookcases were formerly within the archway, she incorporated a painted scene—"I treated it like a little balcony with a railing, and the view I imagined is from a window of the ballroom."

"This hall (opposite) was so architecturally strong, with its massive beamed ceiling, that we felt the furnishings must fit the background," explains John Drews of McMillen, Inc. The Louis XIII–style Savonnerie rug from F. J. Hakamian was chosen as much for its design as for the fact that John knew it could withstand the traffic in the hall. The bronze was used for scale, and the blue in the painting echoes the blue ribbons of the rug. Drews worked with Steven Jonas on the extraordinary window treatment of the two-story Gothic-style window.

A master practitioner of trompe l'oeil for twenty years, Luis P. Molina was instrumental in popularizing the technique. This hall was inspired by an actual room in the Hôtel Carnavalet, a city museum of Paris, painted by François Boucher, assisted by Jean-Honoré Fragonard and Jean-Baptiste Huet.

"This hall was an incredible challenge. Not only was it in terrible shape and a very narrow space, but all of the other designers and their workmen had to pass through it. I ended up working on it in the evenings, after everyone else had left," remembers Luis.

Motivated by the style of the Luckenbach family, the builders of this 1920s house *(overleaf)*, designers Jerry Katz and Linda Goodman replicated a celestial theme in keeping with those stargazing shippers. The original astrological bronze medallions were reset into a new wood floor, surrounded by trompe l'oeil marquetry that conceptually and visually extends the motif. The late-eighteenth-century globe and planetary model sit opposite the photo silkscreen reproduction of the Louvre tapestry, *Maximillian's Hunt*, appropriate mythological and historical threads that serve to unify this eclectic entrance.

18

LIVING ROOMS

The aesthetic core of any showcase house is inevitably the living room. This room, whether it is in a private home or a showcase house, has always represented the structure's major design statement. Whether it's called the parlor, sitting room, or drawing room, it has maintained its image as the formal and most central part of the interior. Although the definition of a living room has begun to blur as this room takes on myriad functions, primarily due to lack of space, most designers would agree that this is still where the major portion of a client's budget is spent. The living room is where the special pieces—the collections, the better paintings, the finer fabrics and antiques—are found. The challenge, as designer Albert Hadley of Parish-Hadley has said, is to make this room comfortable.

Being presented the opportunity to transform a living room in a showcase house may be the pinnacle of a designer's career. Competition can be intense for these rooms, for they are often the leading draw of a showhouse. They represent a distinctiveness and diversity of decorating styles and ideas and an exuberance of imagination that few rooms in a showhouse can match. This is where the stars shine, where the more established designers can express their creative ingenuity, and where younger designers are sometimes given the opportunity to enhance a burgeoning reputation. A showcase house enables the public to see an unfettered Robert K. Lewis push himself to the limit, designing a room with a historical viewpoint yet remaining firmly in the present with comfortable down-filled seating. It's also an opportunity to view the best of Mark Hampton, as he transforms the living room in a formal town house in the city, or to see what young American designers like Jeff Bilhuber, Tom Scheerer, and Sam Blount are up to, or to discover a designer of the caliber of Ronald Bricke.

Early signs of innovative trends and concepts are often previewed in showcase living rooms. When one glimpses three or four examples of an unusual detail—topiaries, birdcages, oxidized-metal finishes, for example—in more than one room, chances are they herald a new direction in design. Wall treatments—such as Ginger Barber's hand-applied cement and mortar, David Barrett's glazed red walls, or Janet Polizzi's fabric-draped walls—are masterful examples of a current emphasis on the inventive handling of background.

On the other hand, Americans' overwhelming desire for an instant pedigree, combined with an awareness of fine antiques and a fascination with the "mother country," spawned the phenomenal renaissance of the "English country" look throughout the United States in the 1980s. But Mario Buatta, the man credited with its rebirth, has been designing in this manner since 1964. And other professionals remain faithful to this style of design, among them Mario's New York colleague Georgina Fairholme. This Scottish designer honed her craft working for John Fowler in London and her splendid sitting room, shown opposite, is a perfect example of why correctly done English country rooms will always remain a staple of the showcase house.

Whether offbeat or traditional, a personal vision, combined with personal details and direction, gives a living room the special quality that sets it apart from other rooms.

The living room of the Kips Bay Boys' Club
Decorator Show House, designed by Georgina Fairholme in 1984.

The master of the English look in the United States, Mario Buatta perfectly combines all the right elements in a room, achieving a civilized elegance in his showcase rooms. This drawing room, in a Kips Bay house, was filled with sunshine, and to maintain that light, ethereal feeling, Mario glazed the walls three shades of very pale lime green, toned in beiges, whites, and *faux marbre*.

"When I do these things I think of a fantasy client—the way she might live in this room and all the things she might have or might not have—and then I start to dream. After that, I basically put it all together, little by little, and the pieces all fit like a puzzle. By the time the show opens, this person I've imagined is living in the room, the candles are lit, the flowers are fresh, and you feel the presence." This room—with its letters, invitations, incense burners, books, bibelots, and masses of fresh flowers—attests to Mario's belief in personalizing.

Most of the fabrics are from Brunschwig & Fils, and the Stark carpet is one of Mario's favorites. The two gilt urns on the mantel provide needed balance for the gilt Chippendale mirror, and the shelves' English porcelain and majolica—both Buatta signatures—are a romantic frame for the fireplace. The blue eighteenth-century French screen is hand-painted paper; the small nineteenth-century blackamoor table is one of a pair in the room.

26

McMillen, the oldest design firm in continuous operation in America, has been creating distinguished interiors since 1923. Betty Sherrill, president of McMillen, discussed this soft floral room *(above and opposite),* which the firm designed in Southampton one summer. "This is a room I could have seen Cordelia Biddle Robertson, the late owner of the house, sitting in. I loved her and we did the room because of her." Cor-

delia was the author of *My Philadelphia Father;* her husband, T. Markoe Robertson, was an architect. The design firm felt that it must remain consistent with the architecture and the personalities of those who lived there.

Carnations and dianthus abound in the room, seen immediately as one enters this typical turn-of-the-century Southampton house. Lee Jofa's "Carnation" fabric—"the

prettiest carnation chintz there is," in Mrs. Sherrill's eyes—has been around for more than twenty years and is upholstered on the walls, chairs, pillows, and window seat, making a romantic statement. The brilliant red silk velvet, also by Lee Jofa, covers the upholstered chair, complete with passementerie, which sits regally on the black carnation rug. The two Victorian black lacquer pieces, inlaid with mother-of-pearl, were discoveries from Newel Art Galleries in New York. Lace curtains allow the afternoon sunlight to filter gently through the room with its subtle elements throughout of Royal Worcester. The brass bucket, fire screen, and black lacquer table in front of the fireplace are all from James II Galleries in New York.

The arched ceiling—painted in record time by designer Richard Lowell Neas himself—opens up this room so that it looks like a summer arbor.

Indicative of the Victorian period—when chintzes were filled with the colors of gardens and fields to counteract the drabness of much of the furniture—is this timeless overstuffed sofa, with chintz and antique needlepoint pillows. Fabric is used in an ingenious manner: Cowtan & Tout's yellow chintz is box-pleated as a dado.

Neas likes to use a black accent which, he feels, adds a sophisticated counterpoint to the light colors of this Southampton house. Here, he utilizes Victorian chairs finished in black lacquer papier-mâché and inlaid with mother-of-pearl.

The English Queen Anne sconces were bought at Mallett's in London and date back to 1720. Neas designed the Victorian button chair with an accordion-pleated skirt.

Juan Pablo Molyneux, who studied architecture in his native Chile and at the Ecole des Beaux-Arts in Paris, as well as Egyptology at the Ecole du Louvre, designed this opulent room *(overleaf)* for the Irish Georgian Society's showhouse in Washington, D.C. Believing that a room should be elegant, but cozy at the same time, Molyneux warmed the room with the richness of Manuel Canovas fabrics on the sofa, chairs, and walls. "When you walk in," he says, "you should immediately feel at ease."

The ottoman is covered in gray leather and paisley, and it also functions as a coffee table. The sofa is softened with antique needlepoint pillows from Terry Morton. An eighteenth-century Chinese seven-fold lacquer screen from Florian Papp adds an effective backdrop to the room.

Sixteen-foot-high ceilings and dark oak paneling were the first things designers Tom Fox and Joe Nahem noticed when they entered this room at Castles on the Sound in Sands Point, Long Island. The room *(above, opposite, and overleaf)* was originally used as the main dining room, and, as the designers observed, "It had a somber and deadening feeling—even the light coming through the leaded glass windows had a painful glare."

The huge limestone fireplace echoes the dramatic design of the room. The creamy perforated tables of lacquered wood—with an eggshell finish, a metal base, and steel "X-spider" supports—are of an original design by Fox-Nahem and succeed in lightening up the room. The unusual silver "Beehive" tea urn is Sheffield—a wonderful juxtaposition with the English Regency penwork collector's cabinet from H. M. Luther Antiques in New York. Filled with numerous little drawers, it's a superb example of the mania for collecting that pervaded England at the time. The woven straw flask rests on a chromium cigarette case, and the

papier-mâché fish, from the designer's own collection, is an antique child's candy box from Germany.

Bound in black leather, Stark Carpet's "Natura" sisal floor covering is another brightening touch, adding an informal elegance to the room. "Regency Stripe," from Decorators Walk, covers the chaise and other pieces in the room, dressed up with Greek key tape from Clarence House. "We chose this awning fabric because it goes with the leisurely, summery feeling of this house, which had a wonderful games room and great views of Long Island Sound." It also sets these pieces apart from the dark elements in the room. A large George II carved wood gilt mirror forms a light backdrop for the bar, which Fox and Nahem decided to place between two French glazed ceramic lamps. Kentshire's Louis Vuitton suitcase, mounted on the wooden stand, is from the 1880s. Placed alongside the shiny black enamel fan, which was patented in 1914, it exemplifies the designers' effortless blending of old and new.

Hydrangeas *(overleaf)* sit squarely on an industrial flat-black I-beam, which provides "relief from the many layers of precious pieces—the antiques with gold leaf and gesso. We thought it was a nice contrast to wake you up, but it actually aggravated many visitors to the room to see something so familiar juxtaposed with the late-eighteenth-century Italian armchairs," noted Tom. "We also wanted the room to have a sense of humor—the kind of place that *we* would feel comfortable in."

The distinguished black gesso and gold-leaf Regency stands, holding the topiaries on either side of the fireplace, were on loan from Maurice Sasson, the architectural and pyramid prints from Kensington Place Antiques in New York.

32

36

Vince Lattuca's love of the opulence of the 1930s set the mood for this boldly dramatic Southampton showhouse *(above, opposite, and overleaf)*. The designer, a member of the Miami Deco Preservation League who is actively involved in the revitalization of Art Deco buildings in that city, is a leading proponent of that sleek, spare, yet contemporary style. "I love the '30s—it was one of the great American periods. Everything was so oversized and large," states Lattuca.

The custom-designed chairs, made out of bird's-eye maple covered in woven silk, follow the lines of low, free-form furniture that became known as modernistic or Art Deco: clear glass, gleaming metal, and plastic were combined with bleached and light-colored woods. The natural curve of the steer-horn footstool extends the arc of John Garofolo's glass sculpture, which, unlike a glass etch-

ing, is actually cut from 1¾-inch glass that the designer brought back from France. Dried twigs lend height.

Taken from the *Normandie*, a painting suspended from steel cables is one of a series of glass panels that once decorated the interior of the French ocean liner. "I really wanted to capture the feeling of a ship," the designer comments. Popular in the 1930s, the mother-in-law plant (so-called because it never dies) appears to grow out of the bird's-eye maple columnar plant stand, which Lattuca designed himself. The carpet's antelope border surrounds custom-colored bone broadloom.

In the office area of the room, three dancing women comprise the pedestal of an unusual silk-shaded lamp, a one-of-a-kind piece found in SoHo. Standing on the custom-designed writing desk with its leather inset

38

are a Bakelite pen holder and brass and glass inkwells – direct allusions to the dominant Art Deco theme. Steer horns form the backbone of the desk chair, silhouetted against the wooden Venetian blinds that the designer loves to use "because they remind me of the old wooden ships of the '30s."

A glass-topped cigarette table in the center, called "Lunar," comes from Les Prismatiques. The pattern of the zebra-skin tray breaks up the clean lines of the raw-silk chaise longue.

The jazzy red lacquered baby-grand piano comes from the designer's own personal collection, while the bird's-eye maple chairs, covered in a printed cheetah suede, were discovered at a Paris flea market. Brass gladiators hold up the music stand, and a pouf acts as a piano stool. *Man in the White Tie*, a portrait of Noel Coward by Robert Crowel, hangs in the hallway.

Angles and curves unite this room, which Stewart R. Skolnick designed on Long Island for the American Cancer Society. Calling it "Untitled 1984," the designer created a timeless aura with his intelligent placement of natural materials. Glass blocks form a sheet of light at the far end, and the addition of leather upholstered pieces from Atelier International Ltd., placed at angles, breaks up the rectangular feeling of the space; clean white tiles from Hastings Tile enhance the openness. James Makin's ceramics on the mantel punctuate the space, as does the media pedestal, and Skolnick's custom-designed coffee table keeps the luminous quality alive.

This room is not what it appears to be. "In this day and age, the hub of family life centers around such modern pleasures as media rooms and family rooms. Even the bathroom has emerged from its private quarters to become more of the public part of the house. We designed this living area with all of this in mind," says Celia Vogel, who designed this room with Mario Mulea. "Everything in this room is tongue-in-cheek." The laminate fireplace contains a video of a burning log. The tiles on the floor, reminiscent of hopscotch squares, actually represent the elements of nature in their color scheme: white for air, red and yellow for fire, blue for water, and gray for earth. Celia and Mario wanted to create an emotional dissonance by using unexpected textures and patterns to generate tactile and visual excitement, hence this bath functions as a living area. Celia says, "It's a sybaritic environment imbued with contemporary pleasures."

42

Looking down from the staircase into this Noel Jeffrey room, one can see the *faux* limestone wall and marble fireplace by Leslie Horan, highlighted by the William Kent mirror. The Biedermeier secretary from Nile Smith is an interesting visual counterpoint to the green shagreen circular table, designed by Jeffrey. Dennis Abbe's etched-glass fire screen enhances the designer's objective to, in his words, "upgrade the quality of the space."

By adding a pair of curved walls and finishing them in a trompe l'oeil limestone, he was able to give this area a very strong architectural space of its own. The teal velvet drapes, like all the fabric in the room, is by Manuel Canovas; the porcelain fruit baskets add a colorful touch to the Biedermeier table and chairs.

44

Despite the structural restraints of a low-beamed ceiling and too many doors and windows, designers John Craft and Susan Katz realized an undeniable cohesiveness in this Southern home. The approach—informal. The outcome—rich and European. The chandelier from Travis Antiques and the coffee table from the Wrecking Bar tend to pull together the seating area, consisting of two Edwardian-style chairs covered in Scalamandre's "Victoria" chintz. Craft expanded the space by placing mirrors on the fireplace wall. The remaining surfaces were papered in a yellow *strié* wallcovering. The area rug is Portuguese needlepoint. Flowers were done by Dennis Schuhart Designs.

One's eye is immediately drawn to the pouf, custom-designed by Katz and Craft and highlighted by the Cowtan & Tout red damask print. The base of the coffee table is a nineteenth-century terra-cotta Corinthian capital from England. An interplay of contemporary and traditional pervades the room—the tiger silk velvet adds zest to the Regency chair in front of the French commode dating back to the Beaux-Arts period of the early twentieth century; a modern painting serves as a backdrop to both pieces. The botanicals to the right of the draped windows are from Okarma/Jones Print Gallery.

46

"A cockpit for two" is how designers R. Scott Bromley and Robin Jacobsen envisioned this living space in New York. They designed the silk and leather sofa on a very low platform to accentuate the height of the room. In fact, its seventeen-foot ceilings were the reason the designers wanted to work with this room.

They put in a surreal fireplace, consisting of glowing cold cathode tubes, "since it's everyone's dream in Manhattan to have a fireplace." The background of the room—the walls—was also imaginatively handled. Plextone, a liquid vinyl spray, was used in three coordinated colors, resembling a granite surface. Sconces from Charles Pfister for Boyd Lighting were deliberately installed upside-down. Thirty thousand dollars worth of audio-visual equipment on one wall (unseen) allowed one to change the entire ambiance of the room at the press of a button.

With an imaginary client in mind, designer Francis Gibbons created a room that was exciting to do and fun to be in. "We set out to create a character, a living, breathing person to inhabit this suite. He became as real to us through this project as a regular design client. Godfreed–the 'Major Domo' –chased women, collected antique trains, loved classical music . . . and also collected exotics like the live parrot named Flame." The zany personality of the "Major Domo" is reflected in the components of this living room. A close look at the pair of Oriental ancestral portraits reveals the faces of President and Mrs. Dwight Eisenhower. The train set on the trestle that runs in and out of the room, and its accompanying artwork, was designed and executed by Danny Youngblood and Cathey Miller of O.X.X. Studios in Riverside, California. Faithful to the waggish theme of this sitting area, Francis placed two oversized-book coffee tables from Charles Gill of Los Angeles in front of his own rag-rug sofa, matching his original idea for drapes perfectly. Form and function are handled inventively: who would have thought to use the willow armoire as a control center for the train set?

Skillfully understating the Chinese motif, Stephens combined lacquer from all periods without creating a spray-can effect. The red lacquer coffee table, formerly an eighteenth-century Chinese screen, is from Matthew Schutz Antiques; the occasional table, once a nineteenth-century tea tray, is from Kentshire. The Chinese lamp is a temple jar from the 1840s.

This formal living room was intended to be used, not simply admired. As in the enormous great halls of England, the wood in this gray *faux-marbre* Adam-style fireplace is placed vertically. The adjacent coal-stove peat buckets are from Kentshire Antiques. Above, an enormous viewing screen hides behind the *faux-bois* molding. All the paneling and bookcases are painted, exemplifying the "natural art of artifice." The black lacquer coffee table from Charles Gracie is notable for its size. Behind it stands the deliberately exposed media center.

Thomas J. Fleming used personal memorabilia to give a personality to this small dark room *(opposite)*. The corner window seat, covered with silk pillows by Scalamandre and fabric by Brunschwig & Fils; the tile-faced fireplace; and the glass door to the upstairs porch—all contribute to an informal yet lush feeling. Filled with collections of books, art by friends, metal soldiers, and boats that line the mantel, Thomas has succeeded in creating an aura of lively history. The green sisal carpet from Phoenix Carpet underscores a low gothic table from the designer's personal collection. The wallpapers by Clarence House and Hobe Erwin add a delicate counterpoint to a predominantly masculine character.

Designing is a creative joy for Katherine Stephens. "Light and fabric are the most important factors in setting a mood in a room," she says. The two similar shades of green of the Manuel Canovas fabric on the sofa and on the Sheraton-style chairs recall such masters as Delacroix, whose juxtaposition of like colors made his work come alive. The unpaired candlesticks follow the same rule: "I don't like things to match. I like them to relate," Katherine explains.

50

"*Having completed* the 'library loo' (see the Bath chapter) with the men in mind, we decided it was time to do a room for the ladies," designer Friederike Kemp Biggs said about the ladies' leisure library and sitting room *(above and opposite)* that she and Jean Simmers did for the Rogers Memorial Library Designer Showhouse. "It was our initial stab at de-chintzing. While we both love bright floral fabrics, we had the feeling that a change was necessary. We could also feel the return of Victoriana. . . . With the ever-escalating prices of eighteenth-century French and English antiques, we decided that the nineteenth century had something more reasonable—and just as decorative— to offer." The wallcovering is a Hinson & Company linen; this white and pale gray overprint of flowers with its natural-colored background evokes the sand along the Southampton shoreline. The designers also used other subtle allusions to the seashore throughout the room—the papier-mâché and mother-of-pearl-inlaid furniture, for example. Stark's richly colored needlepoint carpet dramatizes the spectacular needlepoint stool from Trevor Potts Antiques. Although a very light room, the touches of black everywhere—chairs, carpet, still-life frames, and japanned screen from Donald Magni— provide the necessary counterpoint.

Incorporating a stereo system into the pickled Italian cabinet from Clifford Stanton Antiques in the opposite corner of the room adheres to the designers' desire to preserve a very feminine quality in the room.

Mark Hampton's early training is very much in evidence in this finely tuned English sitting room. One of America's most literate designers, Hampton began painting water-color interior miniatures as a young man. He went on to assist designer David Hicks in London, continuing his painting, and he then returned to New York, where he worked with Mrs. Henry Parish. He then moved to McMillen, where he designed for six years. In 1976 he established his own design company, recently completing several rooms at Blair House and the Naval Observatory in Washington, D.C., and the formal rooms at Gracie Mansion in New York.

Colors are very important to Hampton, as one can see in this vibrantly colored living room. This black-brown room had great Georgian proportions—nearly a cube. Blue was added to the brown paint, a trick that the late Billy Baldwin always advised when he wanted to avoid a mushy chocolate color. "The mood I wanted to create," Hampton states, "was one of an Edwardian library dressed for summer—but a chic Edwardian library that would be exciting to our age." All the furniture—big, old-fashioned pieces of English upholstery—was covered in a cream-colored self-striped cotton from Brunschwig & Fils. Ivory straw matting underlines the room, and creamy gauze is

used on the window treatments, seen in the upper right corner of the room. Ornamentalist woodwork has been painted vanilla ("I do not like dead white in a room") and succeeds in defining the room's borders.

The landscape over the sofa was painted in Italy in the eighteenth century by Pieter van Lindt. Hampton used Georgian mahogany pieces throughout, their darkness balancing the lightness of the tufted, upholstered pieces and the bamboo. Frederick Victoria provided the Coromandel screen.

The atmosphere in this Mark Hampton living room is intimate and somewhat feminine. Robert Jackson executed the trompe l'oeil prints and watercolors in some of the panels, occasionally imitating decoupage—"as though the lady of the house had lacquered the cutouts onto the wall," says Hampton. The paneling was glazed a very pale sky blue, with the moldings kept in the white of the underpaint. The porcelain accessories represent a collection of Chelsea, Staffordshire, and Longton Hall. The furniture is French and English, in the tradition of English and American houses. The extremely fine commode is Louis XV, and the Hyde Park mirror is George III. The wheel-back chairs are a find from Colefax and Fowler. Victoria and Albert floral chintz blankets the enormous bay-window frames. All the fabrics in this room are of natural fiber, as the designer abhors synthetics. The festoon blinds are made of a leaf-green voile, the bergère is covered in a pale green silk taffeta from Scalamandre, and the small chairs are finished in a wide blue-and-white stripe from Cowtan & Tout.

54

56

Because of the architectural restraints—an off-center fireplace and low ceilings in a room that is 24 by 30 feet—not many designers bid to remodel this room in Southampton. "Strangely enough, when I walked in, these became assets for me," says designer Michael La Rocca. "It felt immediately Italianate—the proportions, the color, even the windows." This led him to adopt a Venetian palette and use of furniture.

The Mediterranean blue-green walls, which appear glazed, are in fact papered.

The eighteenth-century Italian commode—made of burled walnut with ivory and mother-of-pearl inlay—is bordered by two latticed windows. The simplicity of the Italian silk curtains from Brunschwig & Fils is intentional. Completely unlined and pulled away from the window, they allow the light to filter through and avoid masking the view outside. Their striped pattern increases the height of the ceiling. The leaf-motif cornice border is made of hand-blocked paper from France.

"I imagined a room I would feel comfortable in," says Josef Pricci. No wicker is to be found on this porch; the designer envisioned it as a multiseasonal space. Custom-designed furniture in lively fabrics from Rose Cumming radiates a warmth that could endure any gray winter day. The French lead-paned doors offer a triptych-like view outside. The linear pattern of the snappy green-and-white striped drapes is subtly repeated in the antique birdcage. Painted wood hurricane chandeliers from John Rosselli hover high above. Below, the Regency foot benches from Kentshire Galleries are covered in a rosebud fabric. The lamps date back to the eighteenth century; originally they were Chinese vases. The Victorian table base is a one-of-a-kind item, in black lacquer gilded with a floral motif, also unearthed at Kentshire.

58

After designing seven showcase-house rooms, Ronald Bricke is an old hand, but his objective is still the same—to create a feeling of period style and quality, whether in an older, architecturally detailed house or a newly constructed room in a condominium. "The easiest part of showhouse participation is the conception of the design. Usually the problem is selecting from all the possibilities. I wanted this room to be the essence of a light, clean summer day and to capture the feelings of country, beach, freshness, light, and relaxation. The smiles on peoples' faces when they entered this room on the warm days of summer were a joy to see." Gauzy, diaphanous curtains of sheer batiste, with a stripe to create solidity, were the most commented-on pieces in the room and established the cool, summery quality that Bricke was after.

In preparation for this room, the designer pinned a sample of the chair fabric—"Bows" from Cowtan & Tout—on his office wall for four weeks before he made his final selection. Jack Lenor Larsen's bleached sisal squares are understated and neatly compatible with the designer's own wall paneling—done in homage to the Scottish architect Charles Rennie Mackintosh. The Corian desk is also of Bricke's own design. The steel bench from Jory and Harvey Prober in the left foreground is crowned with a woven stainless-steel mesh. Josef Hoffmann's grid wastebasket is, once again, indicative of the designer's ability to integrate the past in his totally modern interiors.

This understated room was formerly a maid's quarters in the attic of a Southampton showhouse. Peter Carlson decided he needed to do something spectacular to lure visitors to his sitting room under the eaves. His solution was a mourning dove, which was allowed to roam freely outside the eighteenth-century Italian Montgolfier birdcage from Tony Victoria in this ingeniously barren yet opulent space. Peter commented, "It is strongly architectural, with the complex angles of the gabled end framing a single window. The vertical column creates a tension that reminded me of the architecture of Luis Barragan—therefore, the horizontal water channel was added as a counterpoint. The raked sand and topiary chair allude to summers and Southampton. The arrangement is somewhat surreal."

The Greco-Roman torso dates back to A.D. 200, its translucent marble emanating a sensual coolness. The iron day bed was cast in New York in the nineteenth century. The pearls on "Diva," the draped silk, were applied through a hot-glue process on Gretchen Bellinger fabrics. It sits on top of Elizabeth Eakins's hand-dyed wool rug, which is laid over Japanese rice paper.

Using a minimum of carefully chosen pieces, Carlson succeeds in bridging the gap between minimalism and luxury. Whereas showcase houses can sometimes lean toward high-glaze chintz and highly decorated rooms, this room stands out by the designer's restrained use of furniture and fabric, achieving an overall effect of spare elegance.

Conceived so that a collector could enjoy a good cigar while viewing his art in a comfortable setting, the smoking room *(above and opposite)* was inspired by two major factors: the house itself, a 1915 Italian-style mansion with good interior detailing and a superb fireplace; and the work that Jean-Michel Frank, the father of modern decorating, did for the Rockefellers in New York. Highlighting the intersecting vaulted ceiling in a slightly tarnished glazed silver leaf solidified the verticality; beneath, the 1958 painting entitled *Zoo*, by Joan Brown reiterates that effect. Two "Shadow" vases by Ron Mann offset the painting's penetrating dark-

ness. The mantel and fireplace were original to the room.

Gary Hutton's substantial geometric inclinations come forth uncompromisingly in his furniture design. Cone and cylinder beechwood legs keep afloat his African ribbon-mahogany coffee table, whose hues are echoed in his leather upholstered sofa and chairs. His panel end tables are covered in chamois and bring the cube into play.

Animal skins are used effectively in the work area. John Dickinson's chair is enveloped in goat. A cowhide cabinet, wedded with lacquer, and the writing desk of sandblasted pine are both of Hutton's design.

"We wanted an unexpected, unfinished look to counteract the stark coldness of this high-rise," Ginger Barber explains. So in this living room *(overleaf)* wrinkled white duck cloth was astutely draped like a jabot, exposing the leatherlike quality of its shiny black chintz lining. Subdued ceiling lighting from LSI, executed by Michael Smith, endows the space with a muted, relaxing luminescence. Hand-applied mortar and cement give the appearance of limestone cornice molding.

The hand-woven fabric by Allen Veness on the pillow and the raw teal silk are the only touches of color in this basically neutral room. The designer emphasized a monochromatic scheme by choosing the bleached wood of J. R. Scott's chaise and twisted column lamp and the texture of the Madagascar cloth on the walls.

61

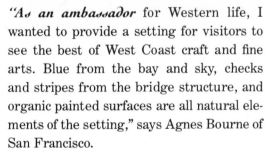

"As an ambassador for Western life, I wanted to provide a setting for visitors to see the best of West Coast craft and fine arts. Blue from the bay and sky, checks and stripes from the bridge structure, and organic painted surfaces are all natural elements of the setting," says Agnes Bourne of San Francisco.

This is a fun room, at once cozy and uncommon. The textured floor was designed to give the impression of width in the narrow space. Halo and Dibianco's radiant lighting in front of the window blazes upward to expose the casually treated drapes by Julia Odegard. Fuller Goldeen Gallery furnished the semifigurative sculpture silhouetted against the walls, whose textured surface was produced by sponging, pressing wrinkled paper against the walls, and pulling it back.

Outside is the bay, inside are the fish: James McCloud of Baker Street Interiors provided the television cabinet, decorated with hand-carved marine life. Once again, Bourne's knack for integrating San Francisco imagery into this room is evident in the close-up of the chair with its hand-painted fabric by Judith Kindler. Its resolute uprightness was intentional—"to keep one alert, yet comfortable; it was meant for conversation such as Quaker ladies would have," explains the designer.

Much-talked about, the whimsical table is representative of new "Art Furniture." A collaborative effort between Agnes and the late Boyd Wright, it is composed entirely of wood—the slate top is trompe l'oeil. A close look at the writing reveals verses by the artists and by George Oppen, the Pulitzer Prize–winning poet.

66

Dan Burton's approach to designing this room in Nashville *(above)* was inspired by "the brightness of life." Fifteen shades of white were chosen to bring forth an uncomplicated elegance to a place that is formal and inviting at the same time. To add warmth, shades of pale pink and yellow were used sparsely on the furniture coverings and pillows. The pewter of the Chinese papered ceiling from Roger Arlington reflects these pastels in a subtle manner. The greatest architectural concern was that every wall was punctuated by either a window, door, or fireplace. This problem was resolved by pushing the sofa and club chairs from Baker Furniture to the center of the room and covering one opening with a large antique bookcase.

"By drawing on centuries of design, we succeeded in creating a contemporary room *(opposite).* It incorporates textures of seventeenth-century Italy, colors of nineteenth-century England, and Japanese lighting techniques from the twenty-first century," says designer Stuart Schepps. He and codesigner Audrey Nevins coordinated diverse materials to produce a rather modulated, masculine work space. Oxblood-red glazed chintz lines the mild-toned green velvet drapes by Fairlawn Design Center. The high-tech table lamp on the designers' own etched-glass, lacquer, and bird's-eye maple writing table restates the vibrant red. Delicately hanging from the ceiling, the silver balls counterbalance the Ya-Ya-Ho cabled lighting system. Underneath, the red oak

floors were ebonized and inlaid with gold lines and white marble diamonds that draw one's eye into the hallway, where *Beach Figures Disrobing* by Irving Aronowitz bathes in light. Stuart explains, "A lot of detail goes into a room to give it a look of simplicity."

A glazed terra-cotta vase made from successive sheets of clay, from Opus II Showroom, sits on a weathered flower stand. Pearl white wall coverings–handmade, with layers built one on top of another, from Friendly Lyon–reflect the gray tones of the room. Near Beth Nablo's huge painting, *Smoke Signals*, stands the bookcase. Says Stuart, "It was a focal point other than art. The needed utility of the bookshelves emphasized the diagonal layout of the room."

68

While maintaining the sophistication and luxury of a beautifully decorated interior, this morning room was designed to suggest the refreshing breezes that flow through a seaside cottage in summer. Splashes of color abound in a spectacular understatement, from the Brunschwig & Fils "Autumn Rose" chintz armchairs to the brightly colored pillows on the sofa. Decorative excess was avoided by designers Marie Johnston and Benn Theodore II. In order to preserve the distinct grandeur of Endean, the former Bird family estate in Boston dating from the 1840s, Theodore explains, "We designed an open space without clutter and distraction." The low table's graceful simplicity is echoed by the white in the subtle harmony of colors of the beach painting by Boston artist Candace Whittemore Lovely.

The English clover ottoman in the foreground of the smaller anteroom was altered to accommodate an American's taste. "We sleeked it down, boxed it, and avoided using fringe to give it a cleaner look," comments Theodore, who custom-made all the furniture. The cloud insert in the ceiling, done by Dorothy Gunther, and the simplicity of the sisal carpet open up an already airy atmosphere. Brunschwig & Fils cabana-stripe fabric covers the armchair, and its detailing on the banquette and pillow adds a fine touch of continuity.

Originally the billiard room of Cobble Court, a large home on Long Island, this intimate and humorous sitting room *(below)* was created by designer David Barrett to be a place to relax after croquet or polo—sports typical of Long Island's "Gold Coast." Playing on the color red, David gave the room a comfortable yet lush look by glazing the walls and stenciling the stained floors. He achieved a restful atmosphere in what he calls the "hunt room" by using a Boussac paisley fabric on the ceiling, drapes, and furniture; a warm Bessarabian rug from Stark Carpet; antiques with a hunt motif; and Second Empire furniture from the designer's own collection. The striking "chaperone's chair" in the foreground, also covered in paisley, is a copy of a French original.

Janet Polizzi wanted to evoke a pastoral feeling in this rather long room *(opposite)*. "I took the room as it was and did the most I could with it. The original vanilla walls were duller than dishwater." She remedied this by placing green moiré Scalamandre drapes over portions of the walls and the doorways (the golden drapes were original to the room).

The faded quality of the Turkish Oushak rug provides a quiet anchor to the fireside seating space. The red-over-black lacquered coffee table, from Rose Tarlow, is a polished counterpoint. Next to the velvet sofa, designed by Janet, a nineteenth-century French black granite and gilt occasional table from Guéridon Antiques holds a crystal ball in a bronze doré setting.

70

73

Suitability and comfort are the best words to describe this gentleman's sitting room for the Opera Delaware Showhouse. Although Marshall R. Taylor Biddle used Lee Jofa's soft yellow fabric, a rich masculine air was achieved through nineteenth-century subtlety.

The "Doeskin" carpet from Rosecore is a pleasing accompaniment to the superb William IV rosewood center table (circa 1825), inlaid with Boulle marquetry, and the small rosewood Regency table.

The careful placement of the horse painting and John Beisel's barn painting above the sofa "provides one of the focal points of balance and symmetry in the room," says Mr. Biddle. The Hansen swing-arm wall lamps and the Directoire hanging lamp cast a glow over the Charles X day bed and the Empire barrel-back chair.

74

This enormous room, which measured 60 by 32 feet, held many possibilities for San Francisco designers Craig Leavitt and Stephen Weaver. While respecting the original décor of Catherine Wagner's interior, they created a truly contemporary room.

The designers' own "spear" table in leather and gold complements the tiger silk velvet love seat. Gold-leaf "flashbacks," holding open the gray silk curtains by J. Robert Scott, were inspired by the flaming sash of an immortal in a Chinese embroidery.

The effect of the Danish Louis XVI-style armchair from Charles Gaylord Antiques behind the gold and lacquered "shaped" metal writing table is boldly eclectic. However, the pairing of the 1920s silver and crystal frond chandelier (original to the room) with the arched console mirror (whose reeded columns are bound in gilded leather) is more conventional.

76

With three enormous windows, the parlor was the most balanced room of this Southampton house. But facing east, it lacked sun for most of the day. Peter van Hattum's strategy was to design a room that would be "the perfect place to spend the evening, to have a brandy after dinner, to play some cards, to smoke a cigar—frankly, a room tending toward the masculine, where a woman would love to be a guest, just as men seem to love being in the feminine surroundings of a frilly and chintzy boudoir." Instead of applying a striped motif to the walls, "something that would have been utterly Regency," van Hattum decided to incorporate a paisley fabric by Brunschwig & Fils to create a softer effect and develop a pattern, and ultimately to make the room more cozy.

The sofa was designed especially for the room, and, although it is much higher off the ground to suit Western tastes and postures, it evokes mosque tearooms, where comfortable divans were adorned with large pillows. The Bessarabian rug from Rosecore Carpet accommodates the leopard skin that graces the Regency "bench" ottoman from David Kerr Antiques in London. Black ebony knobs embellish the Regency rosewood cabinet, now used as a bar. The post-Revolutionary style that conquered Britain and the United States is equally visible in the bull's-eye mirror above the fireplace. The late-eighteenth-century painted chairs, unusual in their time, encircle the Adam-style brass-and-leather tea table, another stylistic anomaly that does indeed work, thanks to van Hattum's knowing hand.

The garden room in Greenwich is a seemingly effortless space that inspires ornithological fantasies. Birds, both real and decorative, fill the room. In a corner sits a green "obelisk" birdcage from John Rosselli Antiques; against the enormous window stands a birdhouse, an English folly from Trevor Potts; there are even two occasional tables whose bases resemble wading cranes. John Robert Moore III used an unusual magnolia chintz from Lee Jofa to cover the couch and pillows. As a final touch, Lee Jofa's delicate gauze allows a soft summer light to filter through.

Suggestions of a Far Eastern leitmotif appear throughout the room: the bentwood and the dark wood tables flank either side of the sofa, enlivened by the two porcelain lamps whose shades are intricately cut in a foliaceous pattern, all from the designer's personal collection. "The feeling I wanted was one of luxury and comfort combined – beautiful furniture in a room filled with plants and flowers. Too often a garden room is a place relegated to house wicker furniture," he notes. Here, though, the English countryside meets the Orient in a serene setting.

Designer, importer, collector, and dealer in antiques, Mary Dial magically transformed this 16-by-16-foot space into a collector's sitting room. Using pieces and furniture from the past, she succeeded in recapturing a romantic spirit with a heroic flavor. Two nineteenth-century French officer's campaign beds were converted into facing couches. Between them sits the coffee table, painted by Timothy Snell; it is finished in aluminum and silver leaf. The Mediterranean floor is composed of bronze and silver paint and subtle suggestions of Pompeian reveries. *Objets trouvés* have become *objets d'art*: the two eighteenth-century stone obelisks, for instance, were taken from a gate in front of a country house in England. The large, very early nineteenth-century Italian mirror "was the key. It was architecturally perfect and gave strength to a rather small, insignificant room," Mary comments. Draped in green chiffon, its ornate carvings are actually painted wood.

The twig table is really bent iron, made in England in the mid-nineteenth century. The standing lamp, from Conran's, is ingeniously camouflaged in a bronze-toned paint.

Perched on a knoll overlooking the Napa Valley vineyards, this room exudes a floral vitality reminiscent of the French and English countrysides. "I wanted to complement the setting and gardens surrounding the house," says designer Joe Horan. The country flavor of the room is set by the painting *Horse with Groom*, by R. Lane.

"The rhododendron-stripe chintz by Stroheim and Romann brings a garden atmosphere to this mix of styles," Joe notes. Dhurrie area rugs from Roscoe, spread over exposed wood floors, define cozy and intimate spaces in the room.

"Natural materials were used to guarantee a genuine, soft feeling," says designer Agnes Bourne. Japanese *tokonoma* was the style desired in this study and music room *(oppo-* *site)*. The 1930s cedar shelving and panels were easily incorporated into niches where soft-fold Roman shades conceal sculptures and art. The Ginsburg Collection provided the wooden horse that sits in front of the fireplace, the one trouble spot for the designer: the rolled-steel facing on the front of the fireplace, a visual magnet, was actually placed over a broken marble façade. Two highly glazed violet cotton chintz comforters, backed in black-green felt, were thrown over the love seats, which Agnes designed. Squared off, they add symmetry to the room and balance the eighteenth-century Chinese bench centered between them. Underneath are leather pillows from Knoll International; these can be pulled out to provide an informal seating arrangement.

*A **classic example*** of a silk purse made from a sow's ear, Paul J. Noël's room *(overleaf)* did not exist before he designed it. "I just walked back ten paces, took a look, and said, 'This is what I have to do,'" stated Noël after being told by the showcase-house committee that they wanted a library in a particular corner of this large room.

The space was created by the addition of the left wall, which contains the massive chinoiserie bookcase, and the back wall. The baseboard molding and chair railing were salvaged from other parts of the house and were then finished in tortoise shell.

The semiantique Indian rug, from Fine Arts Rugs in Brookline, Massachusetts, softened by time, makes a subdued anchor for the warm, earthy tones of the Brun-

schwig & Fils–covered sofas and chairs. The "Wheeler House" wallpaper border, also by Brunschwig, balances the tortoise-shell molding and marble-green wallpaper, which Paul Noël created. "One's eye can rest on any area of the room without being distracted by its generalities because all the accessories and artwork were chosen to blend and not become focal points," comments the designer.

Noël found the lace chest, shown in the right foreground, at Marcoz Antiques in Boston. The wooden Chinese horse, originally a temple toy, the ceramic copies of boccie balls, designed by Constance Leslie, and the needlepoint stool all elegantly complement the room's rich colors.

Just beyond the entrance hall of a New York City town house sat this very small, very square room that Harold Simmons designed for Parish-Hadley, where he had worked for twenty-one years. Simmons, now with van Hattum and Simmons, transformed it into a card room. "It really wasn't large enough for a sitting room, so I designed it according to what I thought the room lent itself to. I designed a card table of brass and gold-tooled leather and placed it in the center of the room with an antique tole lamp from Frederick Victoria hanging overhead. The antique set of chips and cards, found at James II, completes the setting."

The antique Adam marble fireplace set the tone of the room, and Simmons used a complete set of Piranesi prints, gilt-framed, to complement it. Furniture was also used extensively to echo this classic style. The orange terra-cotta glazing on the walls was wiped over the moldings to highlight them, particularly the frieze around the ceiling.

An impromptu bar, made of forest-green wool baize laid over a rectangular table, holds crystal decanters and glasses, as well as a hand-painted lamp, while a French hand-woven tiger silk velvet covers a Regency bench from Gene Tyson. Dominating

one corner of the room is an oval gilt mirror from Hyde Park Antiques, under which sits a small carved marble lion flanked by a pair of bronze candlesticks from Joseph Rondina.

Surrounding the table are four white-and-gold Directoire armchairs from the personal collection of Mrs. Henry Parish II.

86

Fernando Botero's *Rosita*, from Mary-Anne Martin Fine Arts, is the focal point of this nineteenth-century English morning room *(above and opposite)*. Underneath sits a Regency sofa covered with ticking fabric, onto which designer Sam Blount has thrown a handsome array of pillows. This, and the sisal matting on the floor, gives the room a feeling of both quality and informality. The vertical and horizontal placement of a wallpaper border lends a paneled effect.

Flanking the fireplace are two Oriental adjustable pole screens lacquered with a chinoiserie pattern; they were used in the eighteenth century to protect people sitting near the fire from having their wax make-up melt away. Presiding atop the mantel is Brutus Cesarius, flanked by two urns in painted tole; originally made to keep cooked chestnuts warm, the urns now serve a purely decorative function. The postcards on the Regency black gilt mirror with a Greek key border "contribute to creating a very personal room," notes the designer. Through the looking glass, one glimpses the sponged Trojan blue ceiling, bordered with another classical accent.

The Grey Craig house *(overleaf)*, a country hunting estate, was built in 1902 along Philadelphia's Main Line after the plans of architect William Price. "The interior was strongly English in design and ambience, as exemplified by the hardwood floors, carved oak and chestnut paneling, and granite and limestone fireplaces," says Stephen A. Weixler, who designed this room with Walter B. Peterson and Michael Simon. The aim was to create a library appropriate to the architecture and fill it with the collections of generations. The result was a room—rich in color, texture, and light—that had the sought-after comfort of an old family home. A close-up reveals a bust of Jules Mastbaum, a prominent Philadelphia businessman and philanthropist (he built and donated the Rodin Museum to the city). An English landscape with a hunting theme by George Armfield rests on the chestnut mantel, flanked by two antique tole urns from the designer's personal collection. The muted tones of the English lounge chair gain vibrancy against the sea-grass floor covering from Patterson, Flynn, and Martin, Inc. The nineteenth-century needlepoint pillow is from Kentshire Galleries.

Robert K. Lewis had always wanted to do a room with a historical perspective, and, when this Kips Bay room *(above, opposite, and overleaf)* became available, he realized that this was his moment. As a reference point he used the Neoclassical period, when Americans such as Thomas Jefferson looked to Greco-Roman ideals and images to form a national identity. Utilizing his plaster casts of busts by Houdon of four American heroes—Washington, Franklin, Lafayette, and John Paul Jones—he designed this room with furnishings from the late eighteenth century to the first quarter of the nineteenth.

Because the room was so dark, Lewis had the oak paneling lightened to its original light brown color. This immediately changed the feeling of the space. Lewis deliberately chose the pale yellow Cowtan & Tout fabric to offset the dark wood. Combined with the sunny southern exposure, the fabric suc-

ceeds neatly in lightening the room.

The bust of Benjamin Franklin overlooks the table with its four Gustavian side chairs. From Coram Nobis Antiquarians in New York, the chairs are covered in a nineteenth-century brocade that complements the Aubusson. Black Wedgwood and an antique silver tea urn join the Coalport cups and saucers on the 1835 tea table from Kentshire. Antique gilt wood tiebacks gather the striped silk taffeta drapes, which are done in period style.

The theme continues in such pieces as the pair of gilt wood Regency armchairs with ram's-head arm terminals, and the large gilt wood rope-twist George III mirror, which fits perfectly within the panel above the sofa. Robert Lewis designed the coffee table, with its marble top and mahogany legs, for this room; the pale silk moiré footstool and the gilt chairs are from Kentshire.

DINING ROOMS

For most of us, the dining room is the least frequently used room in the house, but it is the room that is most heavily imbued with a sense of tradition and ceremony. The dining room is where special occasions are marked, holidays are celebrated, and elegant candlelit dinners and intimate family gatherings are held. It is also the room where showhouse designers can create a sense of fantasy, of gala. If showcase houses are theater, then the dining room is definitely the stage set. The table, the pivotal point in this room, becomes the theatrical jewel box, formal yet never static. Even if the viewing public in a showcase house doesn't entertain on the same grand scale, they will almost always form an identification with this room and take away from it ideas and details that they can reproduce in their own dining room.

Chairs and sculptures, important pieces in any room, take on added significance here. Samuel Botero's vivid table and splendid use of colorful ribbons immediately invite one to the party that is about to happen. And, by acknowledging Bacchus in the hand-painted border, Thomas Bartlett immediately informs us that this is an oenophile's favorite room, one to be savored and enjoyed.

"Dining rooms have always been a part of our culture," believes Juan Pablo Molyneux. "I approach them for either a client or a showhouse in the same way. They can be grand and casual at the same time, but they must belong, must relate to the rest of the house." His room, pictured opposite, exemplifies the designer's innate ability to work with rich fabrics yet never goes overboard.

The drama of an outstanding chandelier combined with a masterful window treatment, as in the Poling and Ferris room, often sets the direction for the entire dining room, yet imaginative designers may be inspired by a variety of sources, some quite humble. Gary Crain, for instance, filled laundry tubs with masses of flowers and used them as the focal point in his luminous dining room.

For young designers, the dining room presents fewer logistical design problems than the living room or bedroom but still provides an opportunity to create a personal room filled with pomp and circumstance, as all these dining rooms are.

The dining room in the Rogers Memorial Library
Southampton Designers Showhouse, designed by Juan Pablo Molyneux in 1986.

For Marilyn Poling and Elwyn Colby Ferris of Interior Impressions, a fresh approach to tradition is far more important than a particular "look" in creating a successful room. Their dining room, done in contemporary neutrals, subtly blends past and present. The contemporary elements include double banding on the dining-table skirt, an acrylic tray table, and a pair of *faux*-travertine pedestals designed by Ferris. The past is reflected in the antique celadon pieces. Pickled wood chairs carved to look like bark are from I.P.F. International.

Fantasy with a touch of irreverence is what designer John Oetgen hoped for–and achieved–in this Atlanta dining room. "An allegorical theme dominated our thoughts for this room," he states. He placed Robert Jessup's large painting *The Search*, on the wall opposite his custom-made wrought-iron Directoire table. On the glass top is a forest of obelisks and candlesticks from Tiffany & Co. The six nineteenth-century Regency-style black lacquer chairs that encircle the table are covered in Brunschwig & Fils' "Commedia del Arte" fabric. Within the niched shelving are trompe l'oeil fruit-and-vegetable serving pieces. Floral topiaries by Terry Alexander were placed in Coalport urns and placed in front of the niches on antique Directoire gallery tables. Above, the scalloped valance was achieved by hand-painting the ivy border on a silk pongee pelmet, a knotty-weave fabric originally from China.

Immaculately pristine linen covers the walls, chairs, and table of this tastefully subdued Long Island dining room *(overleaf)*. The designers, Lyn Peterson and Kristiina Ratia of Motif Designs, used an off-white carpet from Patterson, Flynn, and Martin on the original marble floor. The pale wood of the chairs from Artistic Frame in New York is in keeping with the dazzlingly light feel of the room. The two white side tables on the far end of the room, underneath the flowers, are actually one table cut in half. The bust and pedestal add a touch of history to this polished room.

The skin of a shark's belly, more commonly known as shagreen, covers the dining table of this spacious eating area. "Because it's Southampton, I wanted to keep it bright, airy, and light and to modify it to the architectural detail of the house. But I was determined to keep it formal," explains designer Michael de Santis. Simplicity was the key to his success. A cotton dhurrie rug over the sisal separates the dining area from the rest of the room. Scalamandre's "Pandora" cream fabric on the six quasi-Regency bleached birch chairs is repeated on the wicker of the living area. The crisp cabinet was custom-made for the space; the enclosing niche contains etched-glass window panels by James Palmer. The wood obelisks from David Barrett were placed near the lead-paned window to give the room needed height and balance.

Since there are no windows in this room, designers Tom Scheerer and Jeff Bilhuber took the liberty of mirroring all sides of the alcoves, thereby enlarging the area and adding depth and light. To suggest the out-of-doors, topiaries were placed inside. A maritime flavor pervades this galley-sized space: the circular pattern of the painted sisal delineates the dining space, where shovels and sand in a champagne bucket dress the table. Even the gessoed and glazed Italian Directoire chairs are adorned with a nautical star. Porthault pervades, from the crisp white piqué tablecloth to the stiff valance above the sunshine-yellow percale drapes. Tom comments, "We thought it appropriate to do something French in spirit (in homage to the endurance of Porthault) but as seen through American eyes. We came up with a lunch pavilion in an imaginary American's villa in the south of France."

The painted mirror in *style grisaille* by Joseph Melland is a reflective backdrop to the cornucopia on Joseph Rondina's nineteenth-century pickled commode with its distinctive black marble top.

101

Gary Crain miraculously transformed this washroom into a sophisticated breakfast room, turning the laundry tub into a planter for masses of miniature daisies, baby's-breath, and periwinkles. By intelligently adding eclectic pieces, Gary succeeded in keeping a light, open feeling. On the shelf are tiny antique Windsor chairs and a Victorian doorstep in the form of a terrier. He also incorporated a tole tray and two Victorian beaded obelisks with antique shells inside minute windows, dating back to the turn of the century, when the house was constructed. The barometer from Switzerland, circa 1830, was inspired by the Louis XIV style; and on the table covered in a Lee Jofa floral is a Victorian silver square box, encircled by nineteenth-century hurricane lamps. The antique needlepoint and silk-border pillows lighten the formal graciousness of the early Chippendale chairs.

Trompe l'oeil subtly pervades: the stone floor, the marble baseboard and crown moldings, the stenciled floral print, and the sponge-glazed walls all reflect James Alan Smith's savoir-faire. The soft buttercream board and baton dado are an extension of the laundry-tub surface, which Gary faithfully restored and which, paradoxically, adds a great richness to the room. His main intention when doing this room was to bring the garden inside, and, everywhere one looks, flowers abound. A pair of stone gold-leaf whippets keep close watch over a marble-topped Louis XV gold-leaf console. The Venetian candlesticks, in amber and clear glass, are from the turn of the century.

103

MR. ROBERT HART

The classic showcase house dining room may not have applications for everyone, but it will sparkle with crystal and silver and certainly awe most visitors. This room, designed by Richard Ridge, is a highly successful example, with all the necessary ingredients—including an eighteenth-century Waterford chandelier from Neslé Antiques, crystal and china from Tiffany & Co., and table linen from Léron.

"This room had all the qualities for what I pictured: an elegant eighteenth-century English dining area. I just updated it color-wise." Richard couldn't find a fabric in the shade of blue he wanted, so he collaborated with Tania Vartan and Lynn Goodpasture on the trompe l'oeil damask (seen reflected in the mirror).

The most important ingredient in the classic dining room is the portrait. Here, Mrs. James Whitman gazes serenely over the console table, Regency table, and period Hepplewhite dining chairs, all from Kent-shire. Completing the set are the vibrant flowers, arranged by Susan Kasen.

"Our room (overleaf) is a toast to spring. We started with a box: a small, simple 13-by-13-foot room with no architectural detail. Balanced against a backdrop of Belgian linen awning stripe, the season bursts forth with nature's finest gift—flowers," says designer Lee Bierly, who designed this room with Christopher Drake. Twenty-four French-matted botanical prints fill the walls with a fluid charm. The stripes add depth, as do the *étagères*. The furniture was kept to a minimum, but substance and weight were attained by tenting the ceiling and by skirting the hexagonal dining table and placing upholstered chairs around it.

The designers chose a hand-painted chinoiserie "monkey" chandelier, reflected in the mirror, to add a touch of whimsy to the room.

Thomas Bartlett, having just returned from an extensive tour of Italy and France, wanted to re-create a European ambience on this Napa Valley estate. "I consider my design eclectic and was inspired not only by the size and shape of this room, but also by the eighteenth-century chairs that I used." A clue to the underlying theme of this room is visible under the cornice: the hand-painted Bacchus grape-leaf frieze by Carole Lansdowne handsomely depicts the Napa wine country.

The painted and parcel-gilt beechwood chairs are Louis XV. Signed, covered in ribbed velvet from Calvin Fabrics, and boasting a back panel from Brunschwig & Fils, their beauty is enhanced by the deliberately bare floors, finished in a soft gray stain. Arne Nyback's watercolor is apropos above the eighteenth-century French sideboard, on which stand antique Oriental jars from the designer's personal collection.

The room was done in predominately eighteenth-century style, with the walls glazed to resemble an eighteenth-century

palazzo interior. The window treatment was inspired by Pauline de Rothschild's draperies in her apartment in Paris and was executed by Sophia D'Mar Schimum. The sheer stripe and glazed chintz provide privacy from the street while allowing light to filter through.

"A well-designed dining room has the flexibility for every mood and occasion. It is the room that can be the most theatrical," says Samuel Botero. An ebullient atmosphere radiates around the rosewood William IV table (circa 1885), with a china setting from Spode and crystal stemware from Baccarat. Icicles made from sheer fabric hang in front of the bay windows, while flowing chintz curtains from Manuel Canovas are patterned with oversized mustard and green bows. Florian Papp supplied the Spanish Neo-Gothic table of mahogany with an ebony inlay. The bronze candleholder from El Antiquare softly illuminates the collection of eighteenth-century Venetian boxes. Marvin Alexander provided the glass-rod basket.

KITCHENS

Form and function, combined with a great working relationship between designer and tradespeople, are the secrets to a successful showcase kitchen. Kitchens today are rarely single-function rooms. Instead, they are the heartbeat of the home, often serving as library, office, sitting and media room, cooking and eating area. As a result of these many different roles, today's kitchens also contain special and often expensive features such as computers, video cassette recorders, stereos, neon lights, hand-painted ceramic tiles, and, of course, an increasingly sophisticated array of appliances. Striking a delicate balance between technology and decoration becomes the goal of today's kitchen designer.

A showcase kitchen's emphasis is entirely different from that of a private kitchen, although the end result may look the same. As Anne Tarasoff, a Long Island designer, explains, "A kitchen in a private home is very, very functional; lengthy consultations are held with the client about his or her needs and particular wants. But a showcase kitchen is strictly aesthetic, done for effect and impact." Nevertheless, designer Florence Perchuk warns that if a designer is not experienced in this area, it can become an endless pit. Many kitchens, unlike most other rooms, where the emphasis is usually on fabrics and furniture, entail large amounts of construction in a short amount of time. A full array of specialists is usually called in: plumbers, electricians, sheetrockers, carpenters, plasterers, tile men. Walls are removed, plumbing and gas lines are brought in, and new electrical systems are sometimes installed. It's no surprise, then, that many designers, given the choice, bypass the kitchen in a showcase house. For those designers who do take on the challenge, the rewards can be great, since public interest in kitchens today is intense and the exposure given to a kitchen designer in a showcase house is considerable.

Designers approach a showcase kitchen in various ways. Richard Schlesinger found his inspiration in the lack of space: "I didn't want it to be a typical 'galley' kitchen. Because of space limitations, I spent much more time on the conception of the room—four months to get it all together and only three weeks to set it up." The end result, a small space that looks great, not only fulfilled his goal but is also a perfect example of a room where everything counts. George Constant's approach, on the other hand, was to design a room that happened to have a kitchen in it. "The fact that it was a kitchen was incidental. I decided to ignore the actual kitchen, which was quite ordinary, and worked to overwhelm it." His dictum, "If something is good, play it up; if bad, play it down," is an important aspect of design that applies to any space, large or small, and certainly to any kitchen.

The kitchen in the Castles on the Sound Designers Showhouse,
designed by Lyn Peterson and Kristiina Ratia of Motif Designs in 1983.

Inspired by the work of the legendary Swedish artist Carl Larsson, designer Jeffrey Lincoln used authentic Gustavian antiques and reproductions in the kitchen of this gentle Swedish cottage at the Mansions and Millionaires Designer's Showcase in Glen Cove, Long Island. "When I first came into this tiny room, it was an unbelievable mess, piled high with rusting garden equipment. You couldn't even walk in the place," says the designer. He ingeniously used some of the room's refuse as decorative elements: the sconces flanking the cement-and-brick fireplace are in fact garden trowels, mounted on wood. One coat of paint was applied to allow the rust to bleed through, in order to antique it. The French-shaped window mullions, painted peach, set off the natural tones of the *confit* jars in the niches. Rooted in the past with authentic Swedish linens, yet firmly in the present with country crockery, this kitchen also pays tribute to Larsson's house, *Little Hyttnas*, with its folded rag rugs and its stenciled walls by artist Lee Ames.

114

The coal-black solidity of the Wolf range at the far end of the room is a very workable anchor in this space. Lovingly worn antique linens from Joyce Ames in New York are used as half-curtains at the window. A pedestal from a local garden center adds architectural interest.

From the cool sea-green Avonite countertops to the pale peach commercial carpeting, the feeling in this 8-by-10-foot galley kitchen *(opposite)* is functional yet serene. "I had to think in inches instead of feet when designing this very small kitchen," says designer Richard Schlesinger. "We wanted maximum storage and work space while staying with the aesthetics. Usually galley kitchens are boring and work only from the left to the right. Here, it goes in all directions." Richard built in all the conveniences—a washer-dryer, microwave, undersized refrigerator, door-storage ironing board, dishwasher, stove, even a media center—without intruding on the room itself. To remain true to his dictum that he did not want it to be a typical kitchen, he used ground-up quartz crystal (usually seen on the exterior of commercial buildings), had it custom-colored, and applied it to the walls. Not only does it enhance the feeling of the room, but it is also temperature-retentive and soundproof: practical qualities for such a small space.

116

Lyn Peterson and Kristiina Ratia of Motif Designs have been creating outstanding kitchen spaces together since 1980. The heart of this modern interpretation of a bistro *(above)* is the racetrack-shaped table —highly polished verdi marble resting on a bistro base. Inexpensive bistro chairs from Conran's are custom-painted to match. Boat-deck paint was used to simulate black-and-white floor tiling, and this color combination was repeated by Motif Designs' own "Café Tile" wallpaper, punctuated by a Greek key border design.

118

"The kitchen in this turn-of-the-century town house was too large and had to be zoned into three areas. It was redesigned and expanded in the 1930s by Cass Gilbert (the architect of New York's Woolworth Building). To create a blend of old and new, we wanted to combine the style of the '30s — for example, the glass-door cabinets — with today's Postmodern details," explains Florence Perchuk, a leading kitchen designer in New York.

Because of the considerable size of the room, two partition walls were constructed to divide it into the serving/pantry area and working area. Architectural interest was created in the pantry area by the pass-through cut into the center and by the pitched archway, which has been painted wisteria blue.

The work area fulfills most kitchen needs with its stainless-steel sinks, Garland stove, Traulsen refrigerator, and Avonite counters, while the opposite wall contains the bare essentials of the 1980s and 1990s: computer, stereo, television, video cassette recorder, intercom system, and a remote control to open the front door.

George Constant's breakfast room (opposite) is a wonderful combination of seriousness and froth. His creative approach to this newly constructed, boxlike kitchen began with two different scales of First Editions checkerboard wallpaper, done in a viridian green and white. Inspired by the Moroccans' use of patterned tile and the English and American use of chair-rail dadoes and wall panels, the designer cut strips, borders, and angles out of the wallpaper, arranging them in random geometric designs. "And while I worked on these architectural details, my paper hanger cried."

"Absolutely everyone asked about my 'tacky' table—which is actually made from upholsterer's tacks over a painted piece of wood." The new "country Biedermeier" chairs are from Italy, and each is covered in a different-colored stripe, maintaining the fresh "up" mood of the room.

The panel of early nineteenth-century wallpaper from France adds the historical solidity that George was searching for. The ingenious interplay between old and new continues in the colorful majolica plates and Josef Hoffmann grid vases and the flowers and fruit arranged on the table.

"It's our job to make dreams come true," believes the design firm of Parish-Hadley. "Our design philosophy is based on Elsie De Wolfe's maxim of 'Suitability, suitability, suitability.' It's a personal statement with great respect for the architecture." This pantry *(right)* in the Upton Pyne mansion in New Jersey was designed by "Sister" Parish with many of the pieces coming from her personal collection, including the wicker baskets and footstool. Robert Jackson hand-painted the blue trellis on the cabinets; Luis Molina executed the subtle stenciled floors.

From her memories of French countrysides and elegant cuisine come Agnes Bourne's fanciful kitchen *(overleaf)*, complete with its antique pavers, authentic copper accessories, and enormous painted landscape murals. Faithfully restoring the space to its original size, she "wanted the inside to be the outside, like a piazza." There was an intention behind the color scheme: the *faux-bois* doors and window frames were to represent the stone architecture of Italy and France, while the turquoise cabinets were meant to allude to the hillsides. Shelley Masters Studio reinterpreted Venice in the classic fresco murals.

The glazed and hand-dipped wall and counter tiles succeed in softening a hard-edged and severe-looking work surface. The overhead pendant lighting (designed by Agnes and produced by Phoenix Day) restates this romantic theme. As in the kitchens of great French châteaux, the hand-hammered copper sink and wrought-iron cutting-block table are all part of a design that uniquely recaptures an intensely warm European feeling.

A gloomy old pantry of the Rynwood estate, formerly the Vanderbilt estate in Old Brookville, Long Island, has been revitalized into a bright, springlike work space by designers Anne and Karyn Tarasoff. A torn-up linoleum floor was given a new countenance by replacing it with terra-cotta tiles, a popular solution that is both practical and appealing. The existing cabinets were kept and given contrast by painting the inside strips dark green. The original oven, with its stainless-steel hinges and door handles, still functions for warming.

The antique chandelier, a rusting, corroded piece, was wire-brushed to reveal the elegant simplicity of its wrought iron. Strung from it—and adding to the air of country nostalgia—are dried herbs and flowers, antique kitchen utensils, and a wire chicken basket. A homespun aura bathes the room, from the turn-of-the-century American pine table, to the Turkish Kilim rug, to the paper-backed fabric that covers the ceiling.

The designers found their main trouble spot to be the huge refrigeration area, which spanned one entire wall. Its bland door surfaces were painted by Caryl Hall to give the appearance of wood, and *faux* tiles and a floral motif and border were added above. It turned out to be the focal point of the room.

Designer Wendy Reynolds, of Cheever House, took this room in hand and successfully captured the spirit of the French countryside. The crown jewels of this long, rectangular Boston kitchen are the hand-painted vegetables on the cabinets and the painted floor—all done by Reynolds's partner Marilyn Markham. Jacqueline Karch made the tiles by pressing small pea pods, baby carrots, squash, and herbs into wet clay to create shapes for glazing. Picking up on the forest-green-and-cream color scheme is the alternately stained, striped oak floor. Rough textured walls are sun-washed and have the warmth of old parchment. The patina of a fine French cherry work table from Autrefois and a pair of Provençal oak armchairs reflect the French inspiration for the room.

Covered in Brunschwig & Fils fabrics, the seating area near the louvered windows seems to widen the kitchen. In contrast to the soft cream-colored background are the fresh-looking majolica plates and the painted vegetables on the cabinets. The hand-picked antiques and accessories come from Wenham Cross, Marcoz, Fieldstone, R & B, and Fine Lines. By diagonally arranging the green back splash tiles, Markham and Reynolds lend an exciting element to this simple and fresh design.

Designed as an island kitchen, both literally and figuratively. Flamingo pinks and Caribbean blues and yellows add color to a predominantly black-and-white space from Celia Vogel and Mario Mulea. The neon strips and "crayon" wall sculpture are encased in acrylic and are easily installed. The dining table is black laminate with a stainless-steel base, and the cabinet tops and fronts are a screen-printed laminate overlay, a durable solution. The refrigerator, usually the bulkiest and least imaginative part of a kitchen, is handled here in a discrete and ingenious manner: three narrow refrigerators are placed inside the black glass front-faced column, one as a beverage and snack center, one for natural foods, and another as a full freezer; they saved space and gained efficiency. Because the ceiling was very high, the cabinets were stepped in order to create a dynamic interest while bringing down the height.

This kitchen is found on the top floor of The Petit Trianon in San Francisco. "Since the room was small and at the top of a very grand building, I thought a simplifying, contemporary look would work best," says Roger Harned. So he covered both walls and ceiling with canvas, then painted on it, continuing the lines and lacquer over the furniture. The walls became art in themselves, requiring no additional enhancement. The neutral color scheme expanded the visual space, as did mirroring the fireplace flue that dominates the middle of the room (seen on the right behind the column). Additional color comes from the copper and turquoise, achieving the overall feeling of "a quiet desert."

Dan Phipps's design is based on a concern for a simple sense of order to tie together the many steps involved in food preparation. "We wanted to create a place for function with motion. Extremely efficient work relationships are created by a strategically placed central island built around a professional Wolf range," explains the designer. The island provides storage and counter space, while sinks, more counter space, and cabinets along the back wall are within easy reach. The freezer and refrigerator, used less often than the other appliances, are sunk into the wall on the other side of the island; a built-in desk stands to their side. Glass bricks help to define this area, which is a perfect quiet space for checking recipes, making shopping lists, and performing other tasks on the computer. A Memphis "Uno" chair adds a necessary touch of color, while the granite, glass, and ColorCore cabinets create crisp, clean edges to this San Francisco kitchen.

130

This kitchen (*above*) had not been touched in thirty-five years. When Gail and Steve Huberman finished with it, the room seemed to leap out of a Lewis Carroll book. "You can really do something special in a showcase house, if you have some thought and some guts. We wanted to keep the effect of a garden, since this house was in Southampton, and we didn't want to use just any old wicker or wrought-iron kitchen chairs. After scouring the four corners of the earth, we thought, 'Why can't we cut chairs to look like trees and garden pieces?' We found someone in the display district of Manhattan who cut a table and four chairs out of plywood and Formica and then hand-painted them each a different garden scene." They added the artifacts to the table—actually painted lamp bases—to keep the linear feel. Becky Franco's painting hangs on the linen-textured walls, whose effect was achieved by painting first horizontally, then vertically, with a thick brush.

The 1930s kitchen of the Kirkeby estate in Los Angeles (*opposite*) could well have been called sterile—before Ron Hefler and David Graham stepped in. They provided warmth and character to stark tile and bare functional appliances by creating a lived-in kitchen for the staff. A vintage late 1920s Stove King range, original to the house, became the focal point for the designers. Because the ceilings are extremely high, they applied acrylic-backed fabric from Clifford Stephens—complementing the three-paneled French screen behind the range. Eddie Egan and Associates refinished the floors in a distressed ebony tone to contrast with the walls and the other color values. On opening night of the showhouse, the aromas of fresh bread and pies emanating from the oven enticed visitors to gather around the old French baker's table, sit down in the Adirondack hickory chairs from Kneedler-Fauchere, and enjoy simple pleasures in a generous old-fashioned kitchen.

BEDROOMS

The room of dreams, the bedroom, was initially a place where entire families would sleep, often in the same oversized bed. First steps toward privacy were tentatively taken when the Marquise de Rambouillet, bothered by the draftiness of her large sleeping quarters in Paris, created the first private bedroom in 1630. As furniture was created especially for these personal retreats, an opulence of bedroom design began to develop. Some of these pieces—the dressing table, armoire, chaise, and canopy beds such as the *lit duchesse* and *lit à la française*—have remained with us, giving us a design legacy that fits comfortably into our twentieth-century bedrooms, fulfilling our desire for luxurious surroundings against an intimate backdrop.

Incorporating stylistic elements of the past into these very private spaces requires an absolute knowledge of design and an understanding of comfort, as Juan Montoya's dramatic bedroom illustrates. Montoya's background in architecture, painting, and design shines through in this classically inspired yet technologically sound bedroom. Paul Vincent Wiseman's reference to Fortuny design in his draped dressing table, combined with his harmonious use of chinoiserie and Chinese porcelain, shows his understanding of the history of this particular San Francisco showhouse. Clifford Stanton's assured mix of pieces from different periods is a paean to his belief that the finest rooms follow the French example of accumulating the best from preceding generations.

Showcase bedrooms are rarely major architectural puzzles, and designers usually have only one requirement—the bed—whether their room is a master suite, guest room, bed-sitting room, bed-and-bath suite, or child's nursery. As one designer succinctly put it, "Those who love designing bedrooms must be in love with making a beautiful bed." The beds that follow, including Barbara Ostrom's Adirondack twig bed, David Barrett's trompe l'oeil creation, and Harry Schule and Ned Marshall's exquisitely draped *lit à la polonaise* share several attributes, including a strong sense of style. There is also a lushness and quality to bed linens today—whether imported or domestic, cashmere or mohair—that is evident in these showhouse bedrooms.

Today the bedroom remains an oasis, an inner sanctum, regardless of its size or design and regardless of its intended occupant, adult or child. All of the designers have imbued these rooms, whether large suites or tiny alcoves, with a totally elegant and extravagantly comfortable appeal. Mariette Himes Gomez's is an ideal example. A small, spare space designed purely for sleeping, it has a simple kind of lavishness, thanks to the designer's sensitivity, focus, and use of superb materials. J. Allen Murphy, on the other hand, includes everything one might possibly need to ensure a night (perhaps a lifetime!) of complete and utter comfort. In accordance with his belief that a showcase room must look lived in, he has included personal mementoes and objects throughout. Rich and warm, it evokes a certain timeless quality, as do all of these personal bedrooms.

The bedroom in the Kips Bay Boys' Club
Decorator Show House, designed by Mario Buatta in 1984.

134

The understated luxury of Brunschwig & Fils' blue "Verrières" fabric adds the color impact that one comes to expect of any room that Mario Buatta designs *(above, opposite, and overleaf)*. A close-up shows the other essential qualities that the designer strives for: comfort, intimacy, and attention to detail. An attractive nineteenth-century Chippendale mantel *en suite* from Danny Allessandro holds favorite drawings, snapshots, and invitations; the English birdcage is from the designer's personal collection. Pratesi supplied the off-white coverlet, and a Chinese export table sits next to the *chaise courte* (the chair and ottoman), on which George Oake's hand-painted pillow and a mohair throw share space. The Belgian crystal lamp on the Dutch bedside table illuminates the silver-framed photographs, the flowers, small *objets*, and pencil-and-paper set.

"This blue fabric is a favorite of mine," Mario explains. "But every time I've used it, I've always had to put it against white or pale blue walls. No one would ever let me place it against lavender walls. People have never understood that whole English and Chinese porcelain and Delft idea of blue and lavender, which is so pretty. But because this was a showcase room, I was able to do it exactly the way I wanted to."

A Stark carpet ties together this perfectly proportioned, flawlessly shaded room.

A pomander ball of baby roses and cloves *(overleaf)* – chosen not only for its fragrance but also for its simple beauty – hangs from a ceramic doorknob.

"*My design* for a master bedroom and bath *en suite* combines strong architectural elements resembling Mayan temple forms, with thick walls and massive volume, and furniture I designed with rich woods, such as macassar, which were in vogue in the 1920s. I had the walls done in a frescolike finish, creating a mysterious, ancient atmosphere," shares Juan Montoya of this classically inspired bedroom. By bridging the gap between decorative excess and barren design, Juan was able to achieve a highly seductive bedroom (*opposite, this page, and overleaf*). Beige airstone was used for the wall treatment—its circular motif is repeated in the chandelier from Süe et Mare. The Art Deco easy chairs with rosewood trim are from Newel Art Galleries in New York, which also provided the Art Deco black lacquer screen with horses and fig-

ures. The sleigh bed, stool, and desk, finished in black lacquer and macassar, are all custom-designed by Juan. Next to the bed is the telephone table, also of his design, with a built-in sound system. Brunschwig & Fils' timeless "Kimono" fabric helps establish the room's mood, as does the elegantly simple Oriental Sarouk from Stark Carpet. "I love to do showcase rooms because it gives you a feeling of freedom. . . . You can create whatever comes into your mind."

The bath area was an oasis set on a platform. Its oxidized-copper-and-glass tub contributes to the rich atmosphere of the room, while the shaving sink—which swivels on its steel column—adds a touch of clever utilitarianism.

Dennis Rolland calls this "a romantic guest-room on a grand country estate," an appropriate description of a room that posed absolutely no structural difficulties for him. "It already had pretty features, so why change it? It's the same as I would do for a client." Six years' experience with Mark Hampton show in this distinctly American bedroom. However, Dennis also filled the room with pieces he imagined the Gimbels (owners of this estate in Connecticut) would bring back from their travels. The *faux*-bamboo pieces in the room—in actuality maple from the American Aesthetic period of the late nineteenth century—are the bed, dressing table, and rocker, all from the Margot Johnson Gallery. The 1930s dressing-table lamps were discovered at M. H. Stockroom, with pleated paper shades from Charlotte Moss and Co. To soften the corner, Dennis added a painted leather Dutch screen from Florian Papp with a palm tree in front. The Edwardian bed treatment—"Victoria Ribbon" chintz from Lee Jofa—is also used on the curved window and walls. Pratesi provided the bed linens as well as the lining material. Graham Smith hand-painted blue ribbons on the corners of the ceiling and above the fireplace to echo the ribbons and bows of the chintz. The easy flow of Stark's "Petit Bouquet" carpet is balanced by the antique needlepoint rug from Hakamian.

143

"I visualized a late-nineteenth-century house on a trout lake, surrounded by a forest in the Adirondacks—a dream paradise for a Teddy Roosevelt type and his romantic wife," states designer Barbara Ostrom. This Morristown, New Jersey, bedroom is unusual in that pieces traditionally considered whimsical or folksy have been used to create a feminine space. Barbara designed the fourposter twig bed and had it made by Ken Heitz of Indian Lake, New York. The trompe l'oeil wallpaper by Brunschwig & Fils suggests a woodsy atmosphere, completing the references to bucolic America.

The hanging flower basket is actually a gigantic fishing creel, which once held caught trout underwater to keep them fresh. The painted *faux-bois* chest is mid-nineteenth century; both are from Howard Kaplan's French Country Store. Old photographs, a basket of apples, and a French student lamp from Eggs & Tricity fill a snug corner.

The hand-hooked cotton rug is distributed by Stark Carpet. Above the mantel, the twig mirror is lacquered in Chinese red. The peaceful interior is animated by the horned chair, the stone pug, quilted cat, and the smiling, yellow-eyed owl andirons. An especially noteworthy piece is the chair to the left of the desk, made from Confederate army rifles by a soldier in the war. All the vintage Adirondack furniture in the room is from Newel Art Galleries in New York.

146

Two mirror images: these double attic garrets were transformed at the Greenwich, Connecticut, showhouse by two sisters, Lemeau & Llana. When presented with the butler's and maid's quarters in this showhouse, they decided to play on the yin-yang qualities of these rooms.

The man's red room is a delicious retreat, a quiet nook to have tea or brandy. "There was an enveloping feeling because of the sloped ceilings of this garret. But architecturally this caused problems. There was an awkwardness of proportion. That's why we used the alcoves as the sleeping area. It improved and made good use of the odd shape.

We had to cope with the ceilings, too," explain the designers. They swagged and ballooned Brunschwig & Fils' red-on-red "Hardwick" into small sails in a Napoleonic style. In keeping with this theme, a Napoleonic campaign bed, made of mahogany with ormolu and ebonized ornamentation, is covered in a quilted faded navy fabric. Urns and ebonized busts top the corner posts. The important sitting pieces in the room

are two matching Empire armchairs covered in a poison green satin, the caned *duchesse brisée,* and a metal campaign stool (not pictured). The bedside table, with its black granite top and shelf and mahogany casing, is supported by carved gold-leaf and deep green eagle legs. A very rare Russian rug from Doris Leslie Blau strongly influenced the design of the room.

In the feminine counterpart to the butler's room, Brunschwig & Fils' "Haddon Hall" glazed chintz opens up the walls and ceiling, complemented by the silk swagging

of the bed. Michael Tyson Murphy's exquisite hand-painted panels in the alcove were fashioned after the same design as the wallpaper.

Striped cut velvet envelops the rolled armchair, with center footstool and companion chair designed by Lemeau & Llana to echo the *duchesse brisée* of the red room. Rays of sun highlight the circular rose medallions of Lemeau's own Aubusson rug. Delicate Redouté floral prints beside Bill William's painted commode round out this boudoir.

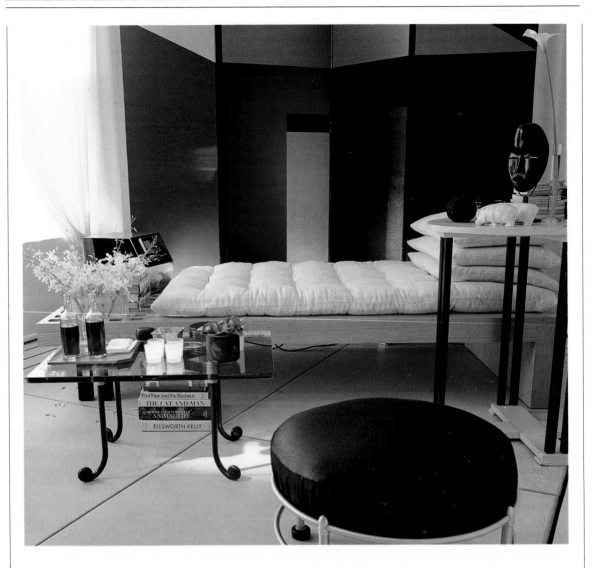

148

*A **designer known*** for his spare environments, Stephen Mallory believes that "when you use a period piece in today's contemporary setting, it seems more honest than pretending that you are living in a seventeenth- or eighteenth-century room. We have the luxury of using wonderful pieces from the past." He illustrates this approach in a small bed-sitting room.

Using Scalamandre's cream wool, Mallory and his associate James Egan draped the walls, pulling the fabric back from the window, thereby diffusing the light and giving the room a sense of depth. They fashioned a pale wool and silk fabric from Yves Gonnett into a futon that lies on a light ash wood day bed of their own design.

An international assortment, all from the designer's personal collection, adorns the tabletop: an ivory hippo from Israel, a black boccie ball from Paris, and a "Dan" mask from Africa. Christopher Chardoff's glass-topped table, inspired by Giacometti, is complemented by the Art Deco stainless-steel and black leather ottoman from Newel Art Galleries. An unusual four-paneled screen, hand-painted on canvas in shades of black and gray, appears burnished by the room's lights.

"Just about everything in this room is trompe l'oeil. It's easy to make a pretty room, but I wanted to do something slightly different, something with zip. I wanted a touch of the theater, of fantasy." David Barrett, a collector of trompe l'oeil, created visual deception without sacrificing practicality. Everything from the *faux-bois* walls, to the polyurethaned pickled floor, to the wooden bed and drapes, can be sponged down and washed.

The zebra skin is painted canvas; the skirted table is covered with painted Celastic; the striped pillows are painted wood. Even the pale green Moroccan folk-art chair, made from bent cypress, has tiny hand-painted leaves growing all over it. "Real" eighteenth- and nineteenth-century trompe l'oeil paintings hang opposite a portrait of the designer as a young man. The box spring, mattress, dark green Chinese table, and just a few of the pillows are the only touches of "reality" in this room.

Albert Pensis converted this space into a bed and bath with classical style. The crown moldings by Focal Point and frieze by Norton Blumenthal are of man-made material that can be glued on easily. The two-tone gray mottled finish of the walls was accomplished by rolling a T-shirt onto the still-wet second layer of paint. The Biedermeier style prevails in the Carpathian burl armoire, with inlaid and etched ebony. The Charles X–style day bed, of inlaid ebony on ash burl, is upholstered in leather. The halogen light fixtures were chosen for their classic simplicity.

Albert wanted to contrast a high-tech feeling with a traditional background. Explains Albert, "People today are very much into classicism but can appreciate that you don't have to exclude high-tech." The electronic tub, a first for American Standard, offers myriad sybaritic possibilities. The water level, temperature, and time of fill-up can be regulated either by remote control from a car phone or from the wall panel, which also features a surveillance system and a complete audio system. The bathtub has a bubble-action whirlpool and gels that change the color of the water. Steps, designed by Albert, cut the tub's height; halogen light floods onto the walls and ceiling, expanding the space.

Albert Hadley and his partner, "Sister" Parish, have been arbiters of American interior design for the past twenty-five years. Their firm, Parish-Hadley Associates, is renowned for "combining pieces from vastly different periods as long as they share an aesthetic honesty of form." Mr. Hadley designed this bed-sitting room *(overleaf)* with "Josephine" (a Parish-Hadley custom fabric and wallpaper) on the walls and windows, set off by the Elizabeth Eakins striped rug of gray, off-white, and black. He then had masterful fun with objects.

The sophisticated wig box (from Mrs. Parish's personal collection) makes a perfect stand for the golden globe, which catches the sun's rays through the French doors. The circular mirror, round vases, and globes are from Mr. Hadley's own collection; the carousel goat and Giacometti desk lamp are also favorite pieces of the designer's. Mr. Hadley's collaged wall—a collection of quotations, postcards, drawings, photographs, sketches, and other memorabilia on a gold framed, custom-made corkboard—completes this very personal room.

Place is also very important to Mr. Hadley. "This room could be anywhere—in the country or in town—but it does open onto the terrace, making one immediately aware of the setting. I believe that a room must have something to do with the surrounding property, whether it be fields, meadows, gardens, or a city street."

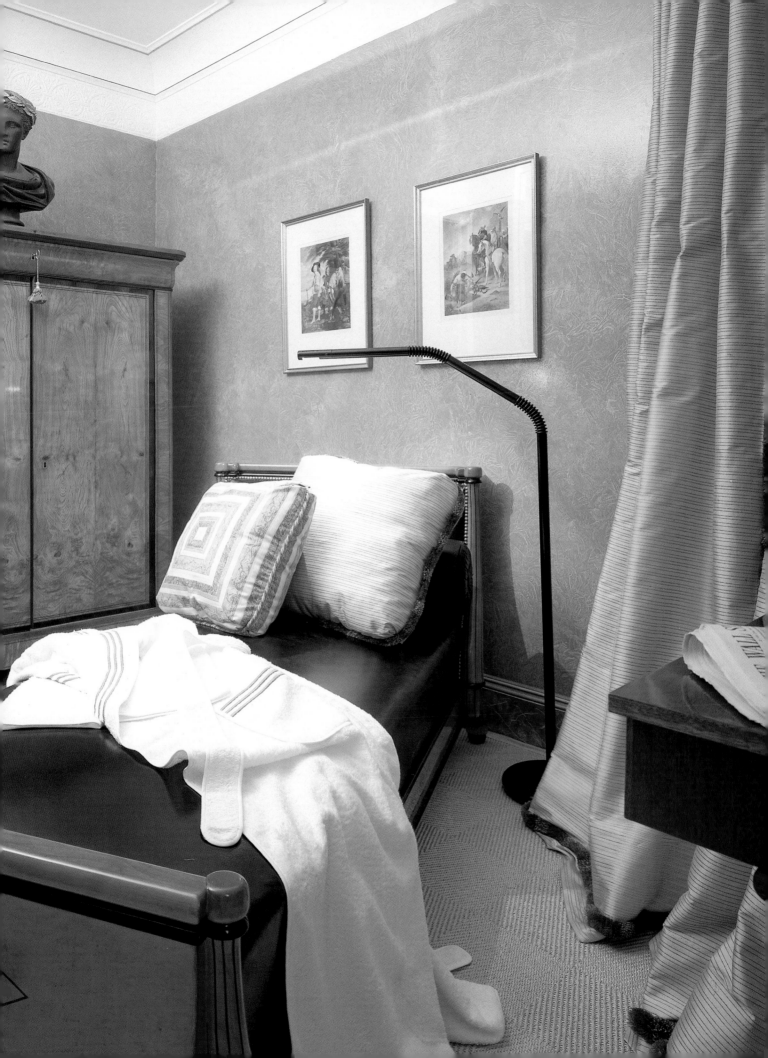

154

Harry Shule and Ned Marshall's celebration of color and romance in this well-tempered bedroom was the result of twelve years of collaboration. "Marshall/Shule isn't known for a 'look.' We design each showcase room with a particular personality in mind, and the room begins to have a character of its own. Everything evolves from that." Inspired by Brunschwig & Fils' wallpaper "Rose Pom Pom," the original of which is in the Paris Museum of Decorative Arts, the designers envisioned this space as an elegant lady's boudoir. Tucked into a corner of a very awkward space in a Kips Bay house is a Louis XVI day bed, painted a pale French gray and covered with Léron linens. Alongside is a small French night table. "Shelly Stripe," also from Brunschwig, is tented over the bed with a trimmed crown, and is caught back with bows at both ends. Harry and Ned ingeniously turned the green-striped fabric into portieres, creating two areas and alleviating the long, narrow feel of the room. Between a matching pair of red glass Venetian mirrors, a japanned William and Mary bureau holds an assortment of found objects and is one of the many pieces from the designers' shop, 1065 Madison.

"Tante Rose," a particularly distinctive brown chintz, covers a small chair in the background. A pair of silver candlestick lamps flanks the dressing table, along with picture frames and silver objects, all from Janet Mavic. A suggestion of whimsy is seen in the English Victorian decoupage screen, which complements the gilt-wood Regency chair with its antique red silk velvet.

A subdued palette was elegantly used in this master bedroom, which Kevin B. Mayo and Ralph De Lucci designed as a genteel retreat. The space was rather large, 32 by 35 feet, allowing the designers to put the bed slightly off-center. Covered in a cocoon of white Battenberg lace by VP Designs, it is lined in a salmon moiré from Boussac of France. The walls are white, with the moldings glazed in a salmon wash, and the entire room is pulled together by the salmon carpeting. The Boussac print fabric used on the draperies is a reproduction of a seventeenth-century pattern. The two chairs on the left —in the foreground a marquise chair from Ralph's own collection, and an eighteenth-century Regency behind it—add architectural strength to this traditionally soft room. And the settee is an elegant spot for afternoon tea, with an English tea table from Charlene Galleries complete with antique silver and porcelain.

156

The personal vision of J. Allen Murphy, as seen in either a showcase room or a room designed for one of his friends, is legendary. A born collector, his rooms spill over with the sort of eye-catching assemblage of *chatchkas* that he is known for.

Allen and his partner, Robert E. Tartarini, designed this Southampton bed-sitting room with the late Cordelia Biddle Robertson in mind. "Since Cordelia was a very whimsical woman and as it was a Southampton house, we did not want to take the project too seriously. We finally had it: a fanciful, intimate, sophisticated jungle just for Cordelia, her dogs, and her friends." The designers used Stark's leopard rug on the floor—dramatic and, necessary for Cordelia's beloved animals, dogproof. Floating a Louis XV bed in the center of the room, Allen painted it red and filled it with undercurtains and linens in Quadrille fabrics, replete with pillows of various sizes, including the requisite "message" pillow. Postimpressionist paintings, borrowed from Stair & Co., hang on the bright pink *strié* walls. The marbleizing is done to look almost like confetti.

A mélange of lions, tigers, and jungle ani-

mals, interspersed with Lowestoft plates, silver, and photographs, sits on the antique English table. In a silver frame is a photo of Cordelia with the actor Walter Pidgeon, taken while they were shooting the film *The Happiest Millionaire.*

158

The dazzling impact of Ann Weber's design is evident in this guest bedroom in Austin, Texas. Her main objective was to make a room that would be enticing in the hot Texas summers, using the coolness of white linen and marble accented with black and gold. Because the owners of the house would not let the designers attach anything to the wall, Ann hung the shirred gauze fabric from the picture molding with custom brass hooks that hung down past the Schumacher wallpaper border. This same border was also used as a baseboard to enliven a very understated background. The elegantly draped ebony and ivory bed is from Pflaster Imports, as are the lion console, floor lamp, and Etruscan vase that give the room a decidedly ancient feel. By placing the bed on an angle and planting a large fern behind, Ann created a much larger feeling to this space. "Centennial" flooring by Congoleum is not only practical; it also adds an illusion of cool marble underfoot.

Piero Pinto, who designed this room, deliberately tried to keep it bare. "I filled it with light woods with black lacquer touches. The wood was tinted to look like cherry. We kept it in tones of peach and terra cotta." The bed, a fourposter Empire reproduction, was made in Italy, as was the rounded "Pozzetto" armchair, which Piero upholstered in black herringbone. "Tulle," a crinkly fishnet-type fabric, was hung to give the illusion of clouds. This room is a replica of the "Rome Suite" at the Doral Saturnia International Spa Resort, which Piero also designed.

163

164

With two unmatched brass fourposter beds from her own collection, Mariette Himes Gomez designed a draped room with a difference. Rather than draping the beds, she hung the walls with a sheer white cotton. In effect, the room became the curtain for the beds. "I've always wanted to put these two beds in a room," says Mariette, "and because it was Southampton and the summer, we deliberately kept the room simple." The floors were kept bare, and the walls were painted shocking yellow. There is no formal window drapery: Mariette simply split the cotton at the window and designed brass tiebacks to hold the fabric. The loveseat, from Corvin Furniture Ltd., is covered in mattress ticking; an Aubusson pillow is plumped on it.

This small room was meant to be a "sparkling aria, not an opera," in the words of its designer, Ronald Bricke. "The glass panels from Manhattan Shade and Glass were the most important part of this room, which was entitled 'Guest Bedroom for a Female Archeologist.' It was their luminous quality that would give the room the sense of mystery and discovery I wanted." Gary Gordon, a young lighting expert, was responsible for the liquid glow of the panels.

To contrast with the glass, the walls were covered with a thin coating of plaster dyed a faint North Sea green. The result was spectacular, and everyone who entered the room *had* to touch the walls. "It was a universal response. I am sure people who hadn't touched a wall in fifty years, since their mother last admonished them to keep their hands off, were pawing these."

Another unique and handsome piece in the room was the Egyptian-style bed from J. Garvin Mecking, Inc., draped in bed linens from Nancy Koltes. This, combined with the truly singular eighteenth-century painting of a Sudanese warrior from the New York Academy of Art, reflects Ron's challenge to himself: "I wanted to see how clear a statement I could make."

The golden sunshine of California shimmers through this terra-cotta dressing room *(above)*. The *faux-marbre* dressing table, dressed in Fortuny fabric and swagged with rosettes, reminds one of the gowns that Fortuny created and epitomize the designer's classically sensuous approach. Paul Vincent Wiseman, the designer of this distinguished room, placed an eighteenth-century Queen Anne chinoiserie lacquered mirror on the dressing table. It is flanked by two chinoiserie reproduction lamps, specifically made for this room. The Italian Directoire chair, mottled with age, refers to the *palazzo* style of the house. The lion legs of the English Regency chaise longue are picked out in gilt. Thirty-eight hand-colored engravings, watermarked 1804, depict early French furniture; the gueridon table, circa 1790, is a find from Robert Demargue.

Paul consulted with a make-up expert in order to create wall colors that would flatter a woman's face. Eleven layers of color were needed — gesso and plaster were mixed together, raked, and then painted by Juliette Klass using an old technique called *plaster strié*.

*A **stark elegance*** pervades this contemporary peach bedroom in San Francisco, designed by Joseph Horan. The sparsely decorated dressing table is evidence of Joe's masterful hand with still lifes. A simple Chinese celadon vase from the Ginsberg Collection, a hand-made bowl, and a reproduction of a Greek bust cohabit with a brass candlestick lamp. A painterly illusion is achieved by the reflection of a bas-relief done by Alan Albert, a local artist, seen in the black-and-white Egyptian *faux*-bone mirror with gold-leaf sun disk.

The size of the room, only 9 by 12 feet, made it difficult to create visual spaciousness. Joseph removed old picture molding, wallpaper, and a corner sink in order to have a straightforward wall surface. He mirrored the headboard and draped it with grommeted, lined canvas, pulled back to act as a frame. This touch accentuated the taller 10-foot-high portion of the room, as well as adding interest and drama. The bed linens are Egyptian cotton, from Lenore Linens in San Francisco. Alongside the bed is a large Grecian olive pot, topped with glass, serving as a nightstand. Seen through the mirror is a planter under the window, camouflaging an old, disused radiator; the lined canvas is repeated for the window treatment.

169

170

Bunny Williams of Parish-Hadley wanted her room to capture the essence of the combination of "*luxe, calme, et volupté*," and, with her creative spirit and an abundant cache of elegant linens, she succeeded. "A Porthault bed is always inviting—the absolute definition of luxury. I created this bed-room to show the linens off." The peach bed set with embroidery, the peach comforter cover, the white piqué blanket cover are all from Porthault—the venerable linen company that, inspired by the Impressionists, first introduced printed linens to the world in 1925.

While keeping with the intent of the room, Mark Hampton transformed this turn-of-the-century bedroom into a clean, refreshing space. The dressing table and hanging lamp were original to the room; Mark simply added a pleated shade of chintz. The chintz, which is repeated throughout, is from Jane Churchill's, as is the companion wall covering.

Mark dipped the bed hanging, undercurtains, and dressing-table frill to make them tea-colored. The original banana-yellow Minton tiles were swagged with cotton batiste—a common practice in homes in the 1880s and '90s. An antique lace spread covers the bed.

The needlepoint rug, set against sisal, brilliantly picks up the colors of the unmatched and unusual seating. The chair at left, which Mark found in London, is traditionally upholstered in two fabrics. The painted chair in front of the dressing table is nineteenth-century Swedish, and the French slipper chair is Louis XV.

172

"This was the sweetest little room. . . . I would have loved to have gotten right into bed." Betty Sherrill, president of the design firm McMillen, Inc., fell in love with this Southampton room that her company designed. Graced by a black iron bed complete with wings ("yet not too overdone"), a Victorian antique yellow needlepoint rug in mint condition, and a Victorian beaded needlepoint hassock (with practical storage space inside), this vibrant room is a delight to be in. Many of the pieces in it come from Mrs. Sherrill's personal collection, including the nineteenth-century red Victorian slipper chair and the perfectly proportioned grandmother's clock. Pink-and-white opaline vases were used throughout, with touches of black lacquer—all complementing the reds, pinks, and yellows of the room.

This room exemplifies Katherine Stephens's desire to take design one step further. Now in the hands of Hunter College in Manhattan, this town house once belonged to the Roosevelts. Inspired by the stoicism of Franklin D. Roosevelt after the onset of his polio, the designer decided to re-create the room thought to be the president's own as a child. "Being disabled doesn't mean that you have to live in surroundings that are unattractive," Katherine explains. She worked closely with the Rusk Institute and Hygia Homecare, which reviewed her final plans. The remote-control surveillance system by Peter McKeon Audio Designs and the sports-model wheelchair from Hygia Homecare help obviate nursing care and assist with daily chores. All the other furniture is easily available through regular design stores: Keller Williams supplied the brass touch lamp and the bed tray, which is actually a cantilevered bar equipped with remote control for the television, curtains, and telephone. A hydraulic-lift television stand has been converted into a night table, its polished chrome readapted to ensure privacy and to conceal medicine inside. The user-friendly adjustable electric bed was upholstered by Aldo Di Roma. Below, the flat low-pile industrial carpet facilitates movement, avoiding drag with the wheelchair; most important, it is static-free. While there are humorous touches, such as the campaign buttons in the shadow box, Katherine says, "I had to know that I could do serious design."

Another tiny room—this one romantically Russian in flavor—Suzie Frankfurt's bed-sitting area in the attic of the Southampton showhouse is a triumph over adversity. The maid's quarters were "small and dingy, but we wanted to make them cozy and wonderful—'a romantic hideaway under the eaves,' if you will." Since the furniture couldn't fit through the narrow doorway, it had to be assembled right in the room.

Suzie achieved her *svetelka* under the eaves with a Stark "Leopard" carpet underfoot and a bottle-green rayon *fille* on the walls. With an eye to the most minute detail, she added nineteenth-century French and Italian drawings from The Artis Group on the opposite wall. A simple lace curtain at the window lightens and elongates this small space. The massive curves of the Italian Directoire chairs and the Russian Empire birch gueridon table seem to fit naturally into these small quarters. The luminescent silk paisley fabric on the chaise longue, the antique silk pillows, and the tufted comforter are all from Old World Weavers.

175

By the age of seventeen, Clifford Stanton was a scene designer, and his early training helped him in his present career in interior design. "Having to express visually what the play is about led me to analyze in interior design what the space is about—and what the people were about." An old hand at showcase rooms, Stanton had a duchess in mind when designing this bedroom. "I came across a photograph of a very chic aristocratic lady in a magazine. I don't remember who she was, but she had a certain air about her that I found interesting, and so I created this room for her."

Filling the room with outstanding, not necessarily matched, pieces from his own shop in Southampton, creating a rich patina of antiques, Clifford also added the ceiling beams, striped and bleached the floors, and ran wainscoting around the room. Center-stage is a *lit d'alcove*, a mid-eighteenth-century transitional-style bed that the designer found in Nice, covered in a quilted Boussac moiré, and draped with a rich print, also from Boussac. The same fabric is upholstered on the walls, in the French style. The soft hues of a late-eighteenth-century rug from Ghiordian Knot in New York enrich the light wooden floor.

176

178

The soaring height of a 19-foot arched ceiling was the major consideration when Glenn Greenstein designed this palatial bedroom in the newly built Dallas Symphony Show-house. "The cornices were designed to reflect the curves in the plaster work and in the furnishings; the tieback draperies ended in puddles on the floor to 'bring down' the high ceiling and to help fill some of the incredible volume of the room," said Glenn. The fabric used for the drapes—a simple plaid Indian silk—is also used on the bedspread and bolsters to tone down the elaborate bed. The king-sized, hand-carved Louis XVI-style beechwood bed is from Orion Antique Importers, and the pair of antique needlepoint pillows is from Eighteenth Century Gallery. A bust of Marie Antoinette sits on the ormolu-mounted rosewood commode. An antique bronze doré candelabra is to her right; above it, cherubs hover within

antique French panels, in a Louis XV-style frame that is thought to have come from the boiserie of a château.

A large Palladian window gives width to this long, narrow room. Additional light is provided by indirect fluorescent light troughs, accented by gold-leaf trim. The Avanti Louis XV-style chair and ottoman with boldly striped pillows unify yet also provide a break from this classical design, while texture and weight are not ignored with Richard Squibb's richly colored tapestry on the sofa. The evenness of the French theme is repeated in the bronze doré fire screen and clock from the reign of Louis XVI. As Glenn elaborates, "I panicked when I saw this room—none of the other designers wanted to touch it. The massiveness dictated light touches to counter the weight of the heavy, sumptuous pieces. So I decided to make it French eclectic."

The English chintz, strié wallpaper, and hand-painted border in Stephanie Stokes's richly appointed bedroom at Chieftains, Connecticut, may be traditional, but the choice of colors is thoroughly up-to-date. "The room was very dark, with heavy branches outside the windows. I chose yellow, which brightened the room and made it seem more cheerful." Structural changes involved removing an ugly wood slab and installing a Louis XVI marble mantel. She also closed up two closets to provide more wall space. Stephanie then added a

dhurrie rug from Rosecore, dyed to her specifications.

The Cowtan & Tout fabric used on the long stretch of curtains and valance covers more than 10 feet of windows and was drawn to scale before cutting. The same floral chintz was used on the chaise, chair, and bed skirt and the wallcoverings are also from this design house. Antiques from Florian Papp, Gina Esposito, Gordon Foster, John Rosselli, Cotswold, and Guild are used intelligently throughout, chosen for what might have been a turn-of-the-century bedroom.

The lines of the late-eighteenth-century framed mirror in walnut and kingwood visually punctuate the sumptuous drapery and dressing table in this elegant, airy boudoir *(opposite, above, and overleaf)*. The intricately carved Venetian shell-motif grotto chair in antique silver finish is from Regency House. Nearby, the floral hatboxes piled high on the Louis XV slipper chair in green brocade evoke a romantic, lived-in quality. Behind the ornately framed family photos is a 1920s lamp—a thrift-shop find—that the designer, Joseph Horan of San Francisco, revamped.

The window of the narrow hallway *(overleaf)* was handled by cascading and folding Quadrille's "Valentine" over a cotton eyelet from Greeff Fabrics. An exquisite counterpoint to the window treatment is the antique wooden Victorian hatbox under a nineteenth-century Irish center table.

An eighteenth-century mahogany butler's tray, which holds a tulip teapot and cup from Sue Fisher King, stands in front of the mirrored closets that covered one entire wall.

184

Seductive yet trim-looking, this gentleman's dressing room *(above and opposite)* by George Constant is full of clean lines and forms, free of decorative excess. A Directoire feeling is created by different elements: the double-crossed ochre/ombre–painted drawers and doorfronts, the arched entrance, and the stenciled-steerhide folding stool.

George sought to contrast this elegance with a certain bold gutsiness. The under-stated neutrality of the cream walls and sisal matting is punctuated by the antique carved alabaster lamp. Practicality abounds: shelves are adjustable to allow for flexibility; open and closed storage areas give easy access; touch latches on doors avoid unnecessary hardware. A dumbwaiter and a stairway are hidden behind the doors. "Some things you just don't want to see," says George.

The common thread that runs through

this award-winning room is unmistakably French—whether in Directoire, Empire, or contemporary style. George achieved this effect more by intuition than intellect. "Everything had to be small or come apart to fit into this room because the stairway leading to it is so narrow. It influenced the selection." The Directoire reproduction bed from Paul M. Jones Inc. is made of brushed steel with polished brass trim; it is outfitted with a simple linen from Alan Campbell. By running hot water and strong coffee over the black-and-white cord trim, George produced a much more subtle beige and black palette that draws attention to the lines of the bed. The black-tiled and *faux-marbre* fireplace was reproportioned by Francis Szczesny. The traditional Directoire stripe appears in the subtle blue-black stool. The original dark oak flooring was scraped and bleached three times; off-white stain and then polyurethane were added.

Against walls of stark white, Deborah Habicht and Ivan Dolin, two young, inventive designers from Long Island, created a gentleman's suite full of their own touches of whimsy *(preceding pages and opposite).* "Our goal was to produce a guest room where everything would be close at hand." After leaving the windows clean—just white wooden blinds with black tape—and putting an inky black sisal from New Directions on the floor, they proceeded to fill up this Greenwich bedroom with objects and pieces they loved. "We cluttered it in a fashion that a real person might clutter it. So many showcase rooms can look picture-perfect, and we wanted our room to look like real life." The mica screen, which Ivan designed, is an iconoclastic backdrop to the carved nineteenth-century oak bed. The bed, along with the chest and the *faux*-oxidized copper desk base, are all from Barnette Shure Antiques.

Two singular pieces that exemplify the designers' great style are the black bicycle-tire mirror and pump on the chest, and the Pierrot lamp from the 1950s (which the designers outfitted with a chandelier and shades instead of the original barrel-drum shade). Although an obviously deliberate mix, the pieces in this room flow with a clearly unifying sense of style.

188

In a small bungalow in the Napa Valley, this space was intended to be a guest room for a wine maker who hosts many European vintners. "With its small ceilings, it was necessary to soften the room up and give it a country formality," says designer Nan Rosenblatt. By using a mottled peach paper from Wallpride, she set the mood: a dry, earthy feeling, reminiscent of vineyards at noon. Built by Sutter Furniture, the canopied bed frame is ruched and upholstered in a polished pale peach cotton, enclosed in an airy off-white cotton voile from France, creating a cocoonlike effect. Beressi's quilting links the diamond motif with the pattern of the white lattice radiator cover. By recovering it in a white-on-white cotton, adding a padded slipcover, and bowing it at the back, Nan ingeniously concealed her own wooden school-desk chair. Close by is an early nineteenth-century Irish pine plant stand, above which is a carved antique pine mirror, both from the Irish Peddler. As a veteran designer of showcase houses, Nan feels, "They offer great exposure, showing the persistence and versatility of the designer. People come year after year, so you have to struggle against getting labeled."

A monkey-faced Napoleon (popular in the eighteenth century) surveys this vigorously martial bedroom *(overleaf)* in Palm Beach. Designed with great wit by Peter Werner, this gentleman's room has a star-stenciled border on its deep green walls and on the sisal rug. The Empire gilt sleigh bed was chosen from Peter's own design store because, as he says, "This is a *showhouse*, so I give the viewers a show." Draped with paisley and animal-skin pillows and corresponding throws, the bed is the perfect foil for the navy-blue wing chair dressed in medals and uniform. Because this room is in a new high-rise with no architectural detail whatsoever, Peter filled it with a cornucopia of military accessories, in keeping with its Napoleonic mood.

191

"*This was meant* to be a man's room. The space was very odd, but its rectangular shape became an important asset when we decided to create an intimate sitting area," explains designer Penne Poole. Colors playing off stripes is the theme, evident in the ceiling and the walls and supported by the white-on-white of the bed. A secondary stripe of black, cream, and blue—on the night table's gathered skirt and black inlay chair—generates a needed tension in this room, which lacked architectural detailing. "The ceiling molding was shallow, so we brought it down from the bottom and ran black tape, while the border was painted white to enhance the mitered effect of the ceiling," confirms the designer. The antique paisley pillows on the bed help to break up the striping, while the classical column creates a portico from the bed to the sitting room. A Hadji Oriental rug reiterates the Eastern touch of the deep blue antique Chinese porcelain vase placed dramatically over the bed.

195

Looking very feminine and very gentle, this blue bedroom *(opposite)*, created by Anthony P. Browne in conjunction with Lil Groueff, was to be a child's room that the occupant would not outgrow as she entered adolescence. By using fabrics from Nina Campbell, Ltd., and Colefax and Fowler and wallpaper from Porthault—all crowned with a vibrant blue ceiling, one of the designer's trademarks—and adding some very special pieces and accessories, they were able to design a pleasant, comfortable room that will develop as a child's needs change.

Madeleine—the enchanting figure of Ludwig Bemelmans's series of children's books—was Benn Theodore's inspiration for this room, and she appears in a print above the antique French walnut vitrine. Very whimsical, very European, and timeless, it is a space where yellow predominates. A Scalamandre floral striped chintz covers the walls and Louis XV day bed; the Austrian curtains, in Swiss gauze, were doubled to tone down the fluidity and to screen out light. Stark Carpet's French needlepoint design coordinates perfectly with the fabrics.

198

"*As a child,* nothing intrigued me and provoked my imagination more than my little hideaways. Every child needs and wants some type of fantasy spot, whether it be a cranny in the forest or a canopy bed." Camille Belmonte succeeded in creating this secret hideaway with her junglelike tree house, complete with hammock and a niche for sleeping. Because she wanted nothing slick in the room, she had the silk trees wrapped in brown, white, and mauve cotton. They match the play quilt (which is pieced together with Velcro) while giving the room a textured softness. The gnarly rubber alligator is also of Camille's design, made from rubberized carpet padding.

"Twig furniture is wonderful for children to dream in. It's whimsical and imaginative, and creates the perfect environment for them." Melinda and Hal Kuehne, artists themselves, conceived this room for a young ballerina, Tiffany Andre, as part of the Bucks County Designer House. Their shop, Heart of America, sells works by artists from around the country, and this room features these wares. The twig bed and cradle were hand-made in Tennessee, while the twig end tables are from Arkansas. From the Kuehne Collection come the wooden dressing screen and the framed hand-made lace tapestries. Pale blue bow stenciling on the rag rug from Folk Art in Vermont is repeated in the design around the ceiling, while the linens from Paper White soften the natural roughness of the twigs.

Not just another circus room, this baby's bedroom is an intelligent exercise in nursery needs. Sallie Campagna, Dot Gomeringer, Debbie Letschin, and Nina Storch—a team of design students from Harford Community College in Maryland—began designing this room under the guidance of their teacher, Carol Lynn Helmkamp, who unfortunately did not live to see its completion. The design concept was specifically created with baby in mind. Bright primary colors were carefully chosen for their stimulating benefits to babies under the age of two. (Research has shown that this color scheme may increase a child's I.Q. by as much as twelve points.)

With a clown hand-painted on the wall, the dressing area is a cozy spot that is certain to hold a baby's interest. The fanciful circus wagon also doubles as a toy chest; it was built by Ron Konkus. An essential rocking chair is in the foreground, and a carousel-horse table stands nearby to hold bottle, bib, and books.

Treating the window like a circus-tent entrance, the young designers flapped back the yellow-lined fabric and added a valance of vibrantly colored dots. The grow chart on the wall completes this miniature circus world.

202

"This house was Victorian in feeling and I wanted to keep that, so I designed an imaginary Victorian child's room. It was to be a little girl's room, but it would have been her older brother room's first; so I used wallpaper and curtain fabric that was neither childish nor feminine," observes Mary Meehan of her Southampton nursery. "The Victorians would have been practical like that, reusing the same things for all the children in the family." She chose a pale blue wallpaper and drapery fabric from Clarence House, with a Brunschwig & Fils border around the lower molding. The floor underneath the antique English needlepoint rug was painted a muddy green. All of the furniture is American Victorian, as are the pictures and toys. The delicacy of the wrought-iron-and-brass bed from House of Charm Antiques in Bridgehampton balances effortlessly with the lace and fringe from Lee Jofa.

Soothing shades of blue are designer Marie Johnston's answer to this twins' nursery in Boston. The mother of twins herself, she wanted a single color scheme—not one color dominating another. A powder blue covers the walls, and a slightly darker blue-and-white Brunschwig & Fils fabric is on the windows. "Everything in this room was custom-made—that's how I decorate." A hand-painted screen by Emilie Henry fills the corner behind the two bassinets, which also contain her hand-painted pillows. Johnston puffed layers of voile around the bassinets and lined them with "Aurora," also from Brunschwig. The low lines of the two custom-made chairs are done in the manner of English nursing chairs. A tufted armchair blends easily into the room; Fieldstone Antiques' stark birdhouse, casually placed on the framed radiator, serves as a decorative toy.

BATHS

Behind closed doors lies the bath—and Americans have not only finally become enamored of this room, but they are also finally allowing themselves to enjoy it as it should be: pleasurable, luxuriant, even entertaining. Americans now want whirlpools, steam rooms, stereo systems, even rotating shower brushes that give one's entire body a good scrub. And companies such as Kohler and American Standard have satisfied the American consumer's desire for well-designed appliances. While not quite returning to the notion of public baths, American bathrooms are becoming, in a sense, social spaces where more than one person can perform his or her morning ablutions without feeling cramped. And, although none of today's baths have quite the heavy drapes and overdone pieces that were common among the wealthy in the eighteenth century, designers today are not afraid to decorate these rooms with swags, jabots, and elaborate tentings when the mood dictates.

Today the bathroom is considered a wonderful small space in which to do some very creative design and to take risks that one might normally avoid. This is a recent phenomenon—in the past a designer gave the bathroom a good scouring, some fresh wallpaper, and some imported towels and was ready to throw it open to the public. But today, as Jean Simmers notes, "If you can't make a bathroom witty or state-of-the-art, it's not worth doing." Perhaps more than any other room, showcase bathrooms are truly exuberant and whimsical. Whether shrouding bathroom fixtures or using a nineteenth-century music stand as a washstand, modern designers stretch the boundaries of traditional design and use the bath to give full rein to their creative powers. Patricia Crane's alligator, Kemp & Simmers's library, and Holden and Dupuy's draped bathroom, seen opposite, each exude a tongue-in-cheek sense of spirit.

Designing a bath in a showcase house requires a distinctly different approach from that needed for most other rooms in the house. Many designers hesitate to take on the expense and rigors of a bath because they're usually faced with two options: either to restore the bathroom to its original state, through sometimes intensive renovation, or to start from scratch and install expensive sinks, heated towel racks, Jacuzzis. Most young, financially insecure designers might not feel comfortable leaving behind a $3,000 soaking tub as they dismantle their room when the showhouse closes. Therefore, experienced showcase bathroom designers generally work very closely with their contractors and suppliers, who often donate their hardware and services gratis. This results in state-of-the-art bathrooms that combine the very latest in both design and technology, allowing the designer to expand on his or her own personal themes.

The bath in the New Orleans Junior League
Decorator Showcase, designed by Ann Holden and Ann Dupuy in 1987.

206

"*We did this bathroom* for purely creative reasons. The starkness of the room is meant to contrast with the rococo feeling in the rest of the house and the overall feeling of the Garden District of New Orleans," says Ann Dupuy, who designed this room with Ann Holden. All the fabrics in this slipcovered *faux* Roman bath (*above and page 204*) are gessoed drop-cloth canvas. But the dressing table, which looks like a drop cloth, is actually tin, done by Regency House in San Francisco. A juxtaposition of styles—the sisal, the eighteenth-century Italian mirror from Milan, the new broken frieze conceived by the designers and executed by Sculptures Inc.—enliven the austere whiteness. A spouting angel is centered between a pair of heads that serve as faucet knobs. Above this arrangement, wooden sconces appear to emerge from the wall. Hands, eggs, a "bust," and a shrouded toilet all contribute a touch of humor.

Faux-*cypress walls,* a tented Pratesi ceiling, hand-painted sisal, and a chalky white bust contribute strength to this gentleman's dressing room in Palm Beach. But it's in the smaller details in the room (*opposite*) where Peter Werner's personal touch really shines: he hand-painted the checkerboard sisal to echo his paintings, or "fragments—as if they were ripped out of Pompeii," on the wall and reflected in the mirror, and he also hand-painted the piece of cement that sits on the aquarium stand and works wonderfully as a sweater table. The library steps (seen in the mirror) that he finished in a *faux* verdigris acts as a vertical "shoe stand." The black leather-and-steel chair from the 1960s, found in a thrift shop, the Swiss batiste held in place with a gigantic nail ("to make the fabric more masculine"), and a brass Empire chandelier add the necessary curves to balance the geometric lines.

209

"We were assigned the smallest room in a very large English Tudor-style house *(opposite)*. We decided humor was the only way to go. We both travel to England a great deal and have stayed in many country houses whose loos always offer good reading material. So we thought, 'Why not a library?'" recounts Jean Simmers, who designed this room with Friederike Kemp Biggs. This "library loo" was so small that it did not allow for proper bookshelves, so the designers used only the spines of the books and brass stripping, which created the illusion of shelves (and reduced the dimension of the bathroom by only ½ inch). Actual book endpaper sheets covered the walls. Glazing the woodwork and marbleizing the toilet were the perfect finishing touches.

Vibrantly striped Rose Cumming fabric engulfs this bath *(above)*, skillfully designed by George Constant. "I wanted it to be gently dramatic and cheerful, especially since it was so small," says George, who describes this space, 7 feet square by 13 feet high, as a "milk carton" of a room. By playing up the height, Constant was able to achieve a pinwheel-like effect. His flair for the unexpected led him to use Clarence House's cinnabar-colored paper on the walls. He also rescued an old bench in the house, upholstered and covered it in a simple chintz and contrasting cording, and thereby converted it into a sophisticated seat. Two Irish mirrors (complete with glass "tears of the Irish") float above the sink. A translucent cotton batiste covers the window, "for softness, and nothing else."

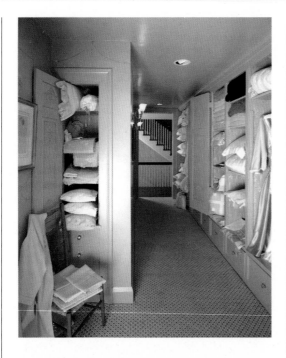

210

Opulent yet intelligent choices were made by Donna Michaels for what she calls the "Heirloom Passage," a linen-filled hallway in Boston *(above)*. "This hallway was an opportunity to use the color gray. It has always suggested to me a level of sophistication unattained by most colors. The shelves were upholstered and piped on all edges for extra wear," states the designer. The hand-painting on the closet doors and wall was done by M. J. Berries, replicated to mimic the quality and attention to detail of days gone by.

"We wanted a house with a turn-of-the-century French feeling," says designer Joyce Jordan of this gracious linen area *(above right)* that she designed with Nancy Batal. The draperies that frame the view onto the gardens of this Boston house are of unlined taffeta from Brunschwig & Fils, crisp-looking yet informal. To the left, French

hand-colored steel costume engravings hang above the *faux*-bamboo table, also from France. The basket of white roses and the limestone garden relic are gentle references to the exterior.

The simplicity of this Adirondack bath *(opposite)* casts its countrified character on the entire room. Barbara Ostrom designed the birch-bark vanity and had it executed by Ken Heitz and fitted with an antique French country wash basin from Howard Kaplan's French Country Store. The antique glove holder, used as a towel bar, is another great find from Kaplan's Manhattan shop. Sisal from Stark Carpet neutrally underscores these natural elements. Two treasures from Newel Art Galleries—the carved Adirondack bear and the bird prints, made from actual bird feathers—add naturalistic touches. This is a room that can only mellow with age.

Looking like his subterranean New York cousins, this wooden alligator at the Vassar Show House dictated the tone of Patricia Crane's bathroom *(opposite)*. The walls were crumbling — hence Lee Wray's applied "granite" finish in natural and everglade green, whose color recurs in the canopy top and back curtains. "Since the 10-foot ceiling was disproportionate to the claw-foot tub, we exaggerated the fabric treatment to add weight," Patricia notes.

The naive mural of a beach scene in this Connecticut bathroom *(above)* was hand-painted by Charlie Mackesy, a twenty-two-year-old English artist. The result was a delightful room of little vistas, masterfully designed by Hethea Nye and Ralph Harvard. Two tortoise mirrors, one a French Regency piece from about 1820, the other a three-way dressing mirror from England, fill the wall. Colefax and Fowler's "Roses and Pansies" floral chintz is used to swag over a sink converted to use as a vanity.

Because this minuscule space (opposite) was tucked away between two concrete chimney stacks, "we had to sheetrock completely in order to create a habitable area." Designers Hydie Hately and Helen Blodgett deftly created a crisp, light, almost nautical room in these cramped quarters. They also added details as practical as a pencil-thin bookcase and a washable rag rug and as personal as the nautical charts from their own travels (which they used as wallpaper throughout).

A small, slightly elongated bath (below) at the Gimbel estate in Greenwich, Connecticut, was subtly brought to life by a bucolic wall mural. Marlea Cashman, who not only designed the room but painted the mural, explains: "This narrow room had a 4-foot-high white-tiled wall, which I likened to a fence in an outdoor space. My painting depicted the rolling hills, open spaces, and peaceful beauty of the Gimbel grounds." Other artistic details also help bring this bath to life—the painted bath tray and canvas rugs by Kathy Whitlock, for instance, and the *faux* burl and tortoise-shell box by Tina Orsie. The eighteenth-century footstool is a perfect spot to leave magazines or to sit and draw a leisurely bath.

215

Carlton Varney's gleeful wallcovering is as imaginative and irreverent as Robert Fiegel and John Gypson's overall concept for this San Francisco servants' bathroom *(opposite)*. The designers recruited a nineteenth-century duet music stand as a shaving stand and designed a wooden butler to serve up toilet tissue. The gas element, originally used to heat water when no running hot water existed, was retained, and it now provides heat for brewing a morning cup of tea. To lighten and enlarge the room, the designers bleached the original wood flooring and then stained it white. The cabinetry and mirror are made of ColorCore Formica laminate that has been inlaid, as in marquetry, to give the effect of rusticated stonework. Since the designers did not want it to be a "powder blue" bath, they used Marimekko's sky blue and white fabric, which also reflects the colors outside. Pierre Sala's modern French chair in red, black, and white is the "sharp element," the counterpoint that they wanted to contrast with the older environment.

Here is a beach-house fantasy where outdoor whitewashed decking forms a staircase to a whirlpool tub. Designer Charles Damga crowned it all with a "sleeping cupid" from David Allan Antiques. Within a semicircular white backdrop surrounded by a light lavender wall fabric, it closes off a window. The halo lighting from Lee's Lighting Studio spotlights the simple beauty of the roses in geometric vases from Hans Appenzeller. The sleek American Standard pedestal has a triangular mirror above it. Luxurious and costly Italian marble, *fior de pesca*, acts as a rich and humorous contradiction to the humble decking. "Because of the whirlpool's prominence in private residences today, it was appropriate to subjugate everything else to it. The cupid is a riveting element that reinforces the importance of the bath. We tried for a singleness of vision—so that the bath has a sense of place."

220

Deborah Habicht and Ivan Dolin originally intended to design this bathroom in vivid primary colors. But the owner of the showhouse wanted a masculine touch, so they ended up working with black and white in three different scales.

The vanity, a 1930s table, is topped with Corian. The futuristic mirror is the designers' own creation, and the chair and lamp come from their personal collection. The slick black-and-white audio and telephone system, from Audio Command, is a testament to the wonders of high-tech.

The textured wallpaper is hand-dragged. Soccer beach balls glow, imaginatively lit from beneath in the sponged tub. Above, a whimsically surreal imitative skylight, created by Becky Franco, houses the stereo speakers.

Fred Bendheim's painting adds the only splashes of color to the room. It hangs behind the center-stage shower, which was entirely designed by Deborah and Ivan, using varying sizes of ceramic tiles and exterior finials that were painted inky black.

"The single most important factor in this room was the fine workmanship of the contractor, Panel Trim," explains Deborah.

This masterfully conceived bathroom is evidence of the late Tim Romanello's appreciation of design. Described by colleagues as an energetic and serious designer, Tim brought an architectural sense to this Southampton bathroom, planned for the Rogers Memorial Library. The crisp lines of Stark's sisal underfoot highlight the touches of brass and gilt throughout the room. A blackamoor table from Rose Cumming, next to a turn-of-the-century pedestal sink from Lost City Arts, holds the essentials. Juan Portela supplied the mirror above. The sofa, almost Moroccan in feeling, gives a personal character to this room, as does the nineteenth-century hotel tub. Made of pewter and brass with a needled shower head, this tub, from Ann-Morris Antiques, adds a subtle monasticism to this superbly designed environment.

PORCHES

Porches and pavilions offer unexpected rewards for both designers and visitors to showcase houses. Designers get to experiment with a totally different type of space. Visitors are genuinely surprised that so much care, passion, and attention to detail have been devoted to these lavish outdoor areas.

Ever since the ancient Chinese and Egyptians, at about the same time, created the first cultivated gardens, we've tried to capture the landscape and bring it inside. Conservatories, teahouses, verandas, pergolas, solariums, porches, gazebos, greenhouses—all attempt to embrace the best of both worlds, the tranquillity of the exterior and the stylized comfort of the interior. With the renewed interest in the pleasures of outdoor living, these spaces have become natural extensions of the home, serving a dual purpose—as outdoor living rooms and alfresco cocktail and dining areas.

Showhouse designers have made abundant use of the colors, smells, and shapes of nature in decorating these rooms, using such devices as floral motifs and chintzes, lattice work, topiary, twig furniture, Victorian plant stands, and so on. Scents from flowering gardens or scattered bowls of potpourri, along with such earthy embellishments as flagstones, pebbles, tiles, and brick, reiterate the union of indoors and outdoors.

Because of the fantasy involved in showcase houses, outdoor spaces usually take on a life all their own. Most designers take their cue from nature and try to reflect the way people interact with it. The late Michael Taylor, known for designing spaces classical in theme but contemporary in application, filled his lush green solarium with a free-form seating area, using his classic "Jennifer Jones" chairs, which are shown opposite. The canopy of ficus that became the ceiling in Maureen Sullivan Stemberg's conservatory has been growing since the house was built, becoming her inspiration for this Northeastern room. Jeff Bilhuber and Tom Scheerer invented a space: their tent grew out of nothing and ended up tight as a ship with overlapped seams, rendering it virtually waterproof in case of a storm. The art of designing a living space in outdoor areas has been refined and elevated by all of these expressive and sophisticated designers.

An outdoor solarium for the San Francisco
Decorator Showcase, designed by the late Michael Taylor in 1984.

225

Reminiscent of an English garden pavilion, pleasing creams, peaches, and greens of this conservatory work as well in the morning light as they do in the evening dusk. Designer Maureen Sullivan Stemberg faced several challenges when designing this space. The cherub—there since the 1930s—couldn't be touched, and Maureen had to work around the climbing ficus in order to redo the walls and swag the damask rose chintz and plaid taffeta from Brunschwig & Fils. "The ficus tree was planted in a hole in the foundation of this house when it was built in the '20s. Over the years it had grown up the inside wall and across the entire ceiling. The responsibility of keeping the ficus alive during our decorating—with the wallpaper glue and polyurethane fumes—was awesome. I had to make the best of it; in fact, it was the key point to the room," explains the designer. Humid or cold days prohibited her from working; damp walls made hanging the Westbury gardens "Ivory Trellis" wallpaper difficult. But, as is often the case in showhouses, Maureen succeeded and the tree survived. The finished space is cozy and livable.

226

*A **bold hand-painted floor*** by James Allan Smith, in black and tan with touches of cream and blue, crisply underlines Gary Crain's summer porch in Southampton *(above)*. Crain used pure white canvas as a canopy to protect against the elements and at the same time succeeded in softening the feeling underneath. A fresh Victorian chintz from Cowtan & Tout covers many of the wicker pieces. Crain painted the sofa a deep green and the chairs a soft brown because, he explains, "they provide a darkened variation to the chintz and mix it up a bit." Such pieces as a wooden lamp from Crain's personal collection, an English pine breakfront with columns and fluting found at Kentshire Galleries (originally from an Irish country house), and majolica blur the line between indoor and outdoor living.

*A **mixture of handmade baskets*** by local artists blend together in this narrow space between a kitchen and a garage *(opposite)*. Designer Brian Killian used acid to clean the red and blue slates, and he stuccoed the walls "to cover up 100 years of cracks, scalings, and all kinds of sins." The fresh colors of artist Audrey Baenziger's palette enliven a two-part screen and an oil-cloth canvas on the floor and also the Scandinavian shelf. The table, "an old country primitive piece," as Brian puts it, shelters a carpenter's toolbox and a jeep-green urn, possibly of Polynesian origin, with raffia ties to facilitate carrying. Lighting filters through the natural pine latticework ceiling—style and storage are the strong points of this space.

230

Early evening summer light, the best of the day, glows on this Southampton porch by Peter van Hattum. "When I got to see the house, it was all boarded up and most of the rooms worth doing were assigned. As I was walking away through a snowstorm, I realized that there must be a back porch. I told Madelle Semerjian, the general chairman,

I'd love to do that space, as I realized that in the summer this would be the best spot in the house. My memories of my grandmother's porch in Holland inspired the entire concept." Peter used "St. James" teal-and-pink chintz from Fonthill, Ltd. on the garden furniture, and he painted the ceiling ice blue for a cool feeling. Starting with a sisal rug from Stark Carpets and wicker dining chairs from Jack Lenor Larsen, he interspersed the porch with such personal mementoes as his rough wrought-iron sconces and coffee table, candlesticks, and green frog. Using generous amounts of baskets and straw on the bar from Victor Karl Antiques, he also put a French wooden milk pail (a hollowed-out birch tree) into service as a wine cooler. The leafiness of the antique majolica from J. Garvin Mecking Antiques is a natural complement to the lush plants and flowers.

"This porch was ultimately meant to be an informal conference area for the Robert Mondavi Winery. But while not ignoring that aspect, we found our inspiration in the hills, shrubs, and Oriental trees that surrounded this showhouse in the Napa Valley," explains Edwin Turrell, who planned this porch with Jack L. Clark.

This outdoor room had to be protected from the often rainy climate of Napa, so the designers began with waterproof canvas. The key border started them in an Oriental direction—a Japanese wedding basket was made into a lamp, and a Japanese cricket cage was hung from the ceiling. Visible behind the flowers and ficus is an antique Oriental gate; an antique Chinese side table is in the foreground.

As they expanded on the design it took on a more eclectic flavor. The coffee table—oxidized bronze rain drums from Sloan Miyasato—works well with the tree-trunk console designed by Mimi London, and the redwood-and-tile flooring by Turrell suggests the geometrics of the Navajo-inspired blanket.

234

The Kirkeby estate's showhouse (preceding pages), sponsored by the Colleague Helpers in Philanthropic Service and the American Foundation for AIDS Research, was open to public exhibit for only three days. Designers Lawn Clark and Gail Hardesty had limited time to prepare their "View from the Terrace." This stone terrace is filled with baby roses, petunias, perennial flax, zinnias, geraniums, lemon and kumquat trees, and braided ficus. Turn-of-the-century French garden chairs, made of wrought iron and cushioned with antique Italian embroidered pillows, invite an afternoon repose. Lisa Bell's paintings on her own easels create an alfresco studio ambience. The French tea service sits on what was once a baker's table. Lavish use of Pratesi linens effectively softens the stone terrace.

Twenty-five-foot ceilings are swept down by arches that are integral to the original architecture of this Southampton house *(above),* built in about 1900. Its second-story porch, as designer Ronald Grimaldi describes it, is "gutsy, with lots of drama. Heavy, strong, but still white, it needed something very large to give it scale." He chose the enormous flower motif of the tablecloth to attain this, a chintz "Delphinium Stripe" from Rose Cumming with shades of white, purple, green, and blue on a gray-and-black linear background. The dark green squiggle-patterned fabric on the seat covers is also from Rose Cumming. Their cool, refreshing tones match those of the porcelain cabbages from Gear. All the wicker is antique, from the Wicker Garden, dating back to the turn of the century.

The "Wisteria Porch," of Georgian Colonial design, was added to Endean, the Charles Sumner Bird estate, at the turn of the century. It stretches 80 feet across the front of the mansion and is framed by a canopy of wisteria. "We based the design of the porch on a traditional theme but with a mix of contemporary, classical, and Oriental styles. "Periwinkle, lilac, peach, and pale taupe were chosen to complement the wisteria and the colors of sunrise and sunset," explain designers Adele Michelin Gross and Stella Mitsakos. The focal point is a hand-painted aubergine sisal rug, on which sits an Oriental "rain table," from a fiberglass replica of the original, that produces an enchanting melody when rained upon. The pair of wicker tub chairs, the chaise longue, and the sofa are strong enough to withstand an entire winter; they're made of fiberglass as well. The buff-colored siding acts as a neutral backdrop to the standing plantation lamp in the form of a banana tree complete with monkeys. The birdcage in front of the window, made by Craig Yerkes, is a reproduction of Eastlake Villa, which was also built at the turn of the century.

236

A ceramic vine clutches a pot containing dahlias and is the perfect detail for this porch. Designer Ronald Grimaldi says, "I wanted to create a cool, refreshing 'living porch' where people can relax, dine, read, drink, and meet in comfortable and luxurious surroundings. The grape motif was appropriate for the outdoors. The colors are easy but rich. Aquamarine mixed with creamy white evokes an atmosphere of coolness, while the purple grapes and green ivy give it the punch every room should have."

The festoon blinds with cotton fringe are made from Rose Cumming's "Grapevine" fabric. They filter the direct sunlight and enhance the sense of privacy as well. "English Ivy" covers the table, set for afternoon tea. Behind is a rectangular wicker dining table topped with hurricane lamps and cabbage porcelain from John Rosselli. Cedar shingles add a warm contrast to an outdoor living space that is as appealing and functional as the indoors.

"This was the most fabulous veranda in the history of verandas!" exclaims designer Josef Pricci. Six different fabrics from Clarence House were used for the tenting alone. Hand-painted peach and blue sisal carpeting underscores the blue and white of the tented and ballooned shades. The big blue wooden coffee table with twined edges, from John Rosselli, is of recent vintage. A white monkey perches on it for no particular reason but whim. "Literally every type of summer flower can be found on this huge veranda," claims the designer, with begonias and Persian violets adding elegant accents of color. The white porcelain dog, another find from John Rosselli, keeps watch over the enormous entertaining area of this Southampton oceanfront house.

240

"*We try very hard* to be good, honest American designers. We tend to steer away from retro and nostalgia," says Jeff Bilhuber. All the elements that contribute to a serene, cool, and summery allure have been intelligently thought out in this tented pavilion *(preceding pages, above, and opposite)*. Muted shades of indigo, coral, sage, and linen were chosen for the exterior of the tent (constructed by Ronald Jonas Interiors) to harmonize with nature; a cool white-on-white stripe for its soothing and calm effect in the interior. Silky tatami matting is underfoot (avoiding the "scratch" of sisal), and afternoon breezes and light slant through the bleached wooded Venetian blinds. Jeff and co-designer Tom Scheerer wanted to design a place that was "modern in spirit, but without trappings of modernism or superhard surfaces."

A screen, covered in an old fabric (de-signed by Billy Baldwin for Woody Woodson and discontinued in the 1950s), defines a dressing area in this 16-by-25-foot space. The designers' choice of accessories – a sandalwood fan, a deck of cards, a birch-bark umbrella stand, a pair of binoculars, and a blanket for a nap – enhances the leisurely summer feeling. The leopard pillows are covered in a Rose Cumming chintz, washed in the ocean and sun-dried on the beach. The black iron chairs and sofa with polished brass finials are available through the designers (based on 1940s Italian *palazzo* furniture) and covered with a hand-loomed Indian cotton (heavier than a sailcloth), while an Indian drum from Taos serves as a side table. The coffee table, designed by Jeff and Tom, is derivative of an Indian hassock. Its turned legs are done in *faux-ivoire*. Leather belting holds the piece together.

This lanai or terrace was designed to reflect the understated elegance and life style of a Hawaiian estate. The curved sweeping lines of the contemporary wicker complement the delicately ornate lines of the house. The palette was inspired by the exterior and its colorful bougainvillaea. Wicker – a common element in tropical furniture – was finished here in black, instead of the more common white. "The black blended nicely with the matte black shingled wall surfaces of the house and also created a sophisticated frame for the contemporary pastel cotton uphol- stery," explain Barbara Cleveland and Frances Y. Gassner, who designed this space. The basic East-West theme of the house is visible in the acrylic painting by Jim Mack and the *tansu* chest and *mochi* table from Orientations, enclosed within the vaulted black archways.

242

A History of Showcase Houses

The Great Exhibition of the Works of Industry of All Nations, held at London's Crystal Palace in 1851, is one of the earliest showcases on record. Its elaborate room displays allowed the Victorians their first in-depth look at home furnishings, *objets*, decorative arts, interior design, and architecture produced by industry. Similar exhibitions were to follow, but none had quite the impact of the Crystal Palace show.

Another important forerunner of the modern showcase house was held at the beginning of the twentieth century, when Elsie de Wolfe, who called herself the first professional woman interior decorator in the United States, designed a house on East 71st Street in Manhattan, with the help of architect Ogden Codman, Jr. Upon its completion, in 1909, Miss de Wolfe invited the press and some friends to see this creation, as C. Ray Smith discusses in his definitive book *Interior Design in 20th-Century America: A History.* Afterward she sold the house, as she declared, "for an encouraging profit."

The prototypical designer showcase house, as we know it today, dates from April 1958, when the Coyote Point Museum Auxiliary in San Mateo, California, organized a house tour in nearby Hillsborough at the A. H. Brawner estate. Each room was designed by a different decorator, admission was charged (with the proceeds going to the Coyote Point Museum for Environmental Education), and the public was invited to see the works of various designers —all under one roof. This house has since run continuously, with the exception of 1980–1981. In June 1958 the Palo Alto Auxiliary of the Children's Home Society opened the doors at the Sharon estate, a thirty-two-room mansion in Menlo Park, California, using the skills of fourteen local designers and contributing funds to the Children's Home Society of California. What began as a unique fund-raising project was widely imitated throughout the country, and today most major cities hold one showcase each spring. Hundreds of urban mansions and country estates have been home to a showcase house, allowing designers the opportunity to decorate in accordance with their own individual vision.

The original Coyote Point and the Children's Home Society showhouses were followed, six years later, by the Junior Philharmonic Committee Showcase House in Pasadena, California. Although in existence for comparatively few years, the Rogers Memorial Library Designer Show House in Southampton is house to many of the top designers. Vassar Designers' Showhouse in Philadelphia was the first in the East, and the Kips Bay Boys' Club Showcase House in New York, almost twenty years old, is now regarded as the most successful in the country in terms of the caliber of design, its "name" designers, and the monies it raises for the Boys' Club.

The beneficiaries of showcase houses are as varied as the rooms themselves. Not only do showhouses raise funds for hospitals, medical research, libraries, scholarship programs, symphonies, and opera companies, they are also very active in the preservation of historic landmarks. For instance, Mansions and Millionaires, held each spring on Long Island, grew out of a concern that the turn-of-the-century mansions on the Gold Coast of Long Island were becoming an endangered species, threatened by developers, neglect, and abuse. The Kirkeby estate in Bel Air, California, although on view to the public for only one weekend in 1987, was a labor of love on the part of its designers, who worked fast and furiously for the American Foundation for AIDS Research and the Children's Institute International, and who still talk about the feeling of camaraderie that it engendered. The San Francisco Showcase raises funds for the San Francisco University High School Scholarship Fund.

Even realtors have realized, as Elsie de Wolfe did, that many so-called white elephants can be primed, painted, polished, and seen by a wealth of potential buyers in a very short time. Showcase houses entered the realm of big business almost from the outset, but, although much attention is paid to design, the importance of their charitable contributions remains paramount. And, without the help of the hundreds of faithful volunteers, none of this would be possible.

Index of Showcase Houses

245

Finding the Right Interior Designer

Confronting the vast array of interior designers to find the right collaboration can be difficult, to say the least. Besides consulting the following list of designers, another excellent way to start the search is to visit your local showcase house, see which rooms appeal to you, and set up an appointment with the designer of that space. Also, many major department stores—such as Bloomingdales, B. Altman, Lord & Taylor, Marshall Field, Burdine's, Bullock's, Lazarus, and Foley's, to name a few—have a staff of interior designers who will work with you. These designers will start by showing you the store's own merchandise and will also help you locate appropriate merchandise from other sources.

Your local yellow pages can lead you to designers in your area; they can also direct you to designer-referral companies, which can acquaint you with the work of many— perhaps hundreds—of designers. These companies offer two basic services. They can show you portfolios and introduce you to selected designers; you would then interview the designers, discuss your needs, check references, and make a decision. Or the company will interview you and select a designer based on its evaluation. Some companies offer both these services, others only one.

Often design-referral companies are willing to work with clients across the country. One of the best, Decorator Previews, has offices in New York, Chicago, Los Angeles, Washington, D.C., and Connecticut (call 800/367-4816 for details). Interior Design Referrals has an office in New York only, but it will introduce you to designers who are ready and able to travel (call Susan Gold at 212/799-7696 for further information). Check the resource sections in the back of many home-design magazines for additional listings.

Professional organizations, such as the American Society of Interior Designers (ASID), have chapters across the country and are more than willing to introduce you to their members. A listing of the major chapters appears at the end of this section. And, finally, there is that old standby— word of mouth.

There are many advantages to working with a designer. First, designers have access to sources that the public cannot use, such as many fine fabric manufacturers and antique dealers who sell "to the trade" only. A designer will certainly be able to supply the services of an architect and may even have an architect on staff. He or she will be able to recognize fire and safety hazards, as well as potential building-code violations, and will be able to steer you through the process of having plans approved. Above all, a good designer will be a wellspring of exciting, inventive ideas.

The key to a satisfying experience with an interior designer is being frank about your likes, dislikes, daily living patterns and lifestyle, and expectations. This is not the time to be intimidated but rather to be completely honest about what you hope to achieve.

Some designers will work on a fee basis, others an hourly rate. Some will retain commissions on merchandise they purchase for you, and still others may combine one or two of these fee structures. Preparing a written agreement will avoid misunderstandings.

Following are the addresses of twenty-nine chapters of ASID. Write to the appropriate Chapter Administrator for information. There are other smaller chapters throughout the country. Contact ASID National Headquarters, 1430 Broadway, New York, NY 10018, for information about the chapter nearest you.

ARIZONA NORTH CHAPTER ASID
3602 East Campbell
Phoenix, AZ 85018
(602) 955-1679

CALIFORNIA INLAND CHAPTER ASID
440 East Holt Avenue
Pomona, CA 91767
(714) 623-2130

CALIFORNIA LOS ANGELES CHAPTER ASID
PDC 8687 Melrose Avenue, #BM-52
Los Angeles, CA 90069
(213) 659-8998

CALIFORNIA NORTH CHAPTER ASID
2 Henry Adams Street, Suite 301
San Francisco, CA 94103
(415) 626-2743

CALIFORNIA ORANGE COUNTY CHAPTER ASID
23811 Aliso Creek Road, Suite 124B
Laguna Niguel, CA 92656
(714) 643-1549

CALIFORNIA PENINSULA CHAPTER ASID
2317 Broadway, Suite 310
Redwood City, CA 94063
(415) 363-1004

CALIFORNIA SAN DIEGO CHAPTER ASID
4010 Morena Boulevard, #240
San Diego, CA 92117
(No phone available)

COLORADO CHAPTER ASID
595 South Broadway
Denver, CO 80209
(303) 733-1441

FLORIDA SOUTH CHAPTER ASID
4100 N.E. Second Avenue
Miami, FL 33137
(305) 576-2739

GEORGIA CHAPTER ASID
351 Peachtree Hills Avenue, N.E., #504-A
Atlanta, GA 30305
(404) 261-2743

GREAT LAKES CHAPTER ASID
1700 Stutz Drive, Space 79
Troy, MI 48084
(No phone available)

HAWAII CHAPTER ASID
1526 Wilhelmina Rise
Honolulu, HI 96816
(808) 734-4797

ILLINOIS CHAPTER ASID
620 Merchandise Mart
Chicago, IL 60654
(312) 467-5080

INTERMOUNTAIN CHAPTER ASID
522 South 400 West
Salt Lake City, UT 84101
(801) 363-4830

MINNESOTA CHAPTER ASID
275 Market Street, Suite C-27
Minneapolis, MN 55405
(612) 339-6003

MISSOURI EAST CHAPTER ASID
P.O. Box 2955
St. Louis, MO 63130
(No phone available)

NEW ENGLAND CHAPTER ASID
132 Great Road, Suite 200
Stow, MA 01775
(617) 897-3784

NEW YORK METRO CHAPTER ASID
200 Lexington Avenue
New York, NY 10016
(212) 685-3480

OHIO NORTH CHAPTER ASID
23533 Mercantile Road
Beechwood, OH 44122
(216) 666-9188

OREGON CHAPTER ASID
2701 N.W. Vaughn, #608-C
Portland, OR 97210
(503) 223-8231

PENNSYLVANIA EAST CHAPTER ASID
2400 Market Street
Philadelphia, PA 19103
(215) 568-3884

PUERTO RICO CHAPTER ASID
P.O. Box 11236, Caparra Heights Station
San Juan, PR 00922
(809) 758-4409

TEXAS CHAPTER ASID
P.O. Box 58525
Dallas, TX 75258
(214) 748-1541

TEXAS GULF COAST CHAPTER ASID
5120 Woodway
Houston, TX 77056
(713) 626-1470

WASHINGTON METRO CHAPTER ASID
300 D Street S.W., #213
Washington, DC 20024
(202) 488-4100

WASHINGTON STATE CHAPTER ASID
5701 6th Avenue South
Seattle, WA 98108
(206) 762-1200

WISCONSIN CHAPTER ASID
P.O. Box 257
Milwaukee, WI 53201
(414) 273-1033

Index of Designers

Every effort has been made to ensure the accuracy of the following information. However, with time addresses change, so a compilation of this sort cannot, despite all efforts, be absolutely precise.

Kalef Aleton
Kalef Aleton et Cie.
882 North Doheny Drive
Los Angeles, CA 90069
Pages 12, 13

Ginger Barber
Ginger Barber Design, Inc.
2024 McDuffie
Houston, TX 77019
Pages 23, 61, 62–63

John Baric
Simonson & Baric
847 Lexington Avenue
New York, NY 10021
Pages 14–15

David Barrett
Fine Arts Building
232 East 59 Street
New York, NY 10022
Pages 23, 70, 133, 149

Thomas Bartlett
P.O. Box 2499
Yountville, CA 94599
Pages 95, 108–109

Nancy Batal
Jordan & Batal Interior Design
One Midland
Andover, MA 01810
Page 210

Camille Belmonte
Decor & Design by Camille
4 Old Meadow Road
Dover, MA 02030
Page 198

Marshall R. Taylor Biddle
127 East 59 Street
Room 201
New York, NY 10022
Pages 72–73

Lee Bierly, ASID
Bierly-Drake Associates, Inc.
205 Newbury Street
Boston, MA 02116
Pages 105, 106–107

Friederike Kemp Biggs
K·B·H Interiors, Inc.
1220 Park Avenue
New York, NY 10128
Pages 50–51, 208, 209

Jeff Bilhuber
Bilhuber Design
19 East 65 Street
New York, NY 10021
Pages 101, 225, 238–241

Helen Blodgett
Blodgett/Hately Design, Inc.
860 Park Avenue
New York, NY 10021
Pages 214, 215

Sam T. Blount
Irvine and Fleming, Inc.
19 East 57 Street
New York, NY 10022
Pages 86, 87

Samuel Botero
150 East 58 Street
New York, NY 10155
Pages 95, 110–111

Agnes Bourne, ASID
550 15 Street
Space 34
San Francisco, CA 94103
Pages 64–65, 80, 81, 121, 122–123

Ronald Bricke
Ronald Bricke & Associates
333 East 69 Street
New York, NY 10021
Pages 58, 165

R. Scott Bromley
Bromley/Jacobsen Design, Inc.
242 West 27 Street
New York, NY 10001
Page 46

Anthony P. Browne
2903 M Street, NW
Washington, DC 20007
Pages 196, 197

Mario Buatta
120 East 80 Street
New York, NY 10021
Pages 23, 24–25, 132, 134–137

Daniel F. Burton
2801 West End Avenue
Nashville, TN 37203
Page 66

Sallie Campagna
Pages 200–201

Peter F. Carlson
196 Grand Street
New York, NY 10013
Page 59

Marlea Cashman
102 Five Mile River Road
Darien, CT 06820
Page 215

Cheever House
90 Main Street
Andover, MA 01810
Page 125

Jack L. Clark
Edwin Turrell & Associates
202 Fair Oaks Street
San Francisco, CA 94110
Page 231

Lawn Clark
Lawn Clark Design
2317 North Beverly Glen
Los Angeles, CA 90077
Pages 232–233, 234

Barbara Cleveland
FG DESIGN LTD.
P.O. Box 1693
Kailua, HI 96734
Pages 242–243

George Constant
George Constant, Inc.
425 East 63 Street
New York, NY 10021
Pages 113, 120, 121, 184–185, 209

John W. Craft
John W. Craft Interiors
3130 Maple Drive, NE
Suite #1
Atlanta, GA 30305
Pages 44–45

Gary P. Crain
234 East 58 Street
New York, NY 10022
Pages 95, 102–103, 228

Patricia Crane, ASID
Patricia Crane Associates
600 Lancaster Avenue
Bryn Mawr, PA 19010
Pages 212, 213

Charles Damga
812 Broadway
New York, NY 10003
Pages 218–219

Ralph De Lucci
Mayo-De Lucci Interiors
405 East 54 Street
New York, NY 10022
Pages 156–157

Michael de Santis
Michael de Santis, Inc.
1110 Second Avenue
New York, NY 10022
Page 100

Mary Dial
Mary Dial Design
One Sutton Place South
New York, NY 10022
Pages 2, 78, 79

Ivan Dolin
P.O. Box 1299
Bay Shore, NY 11706
Pages 186–189, 220–221

Christopher Drake, ASID
Bierly-Drake Associates, Inc.
205 Newbury Street
Boston, MA 02116
Pages 105, 106–107

John Drews. See McMillen, Inc.

Ann K. Dupuy
Holden & Dupuy Interior Design
1101 First Street
New Orleans, LA 70130
Pages 204, 206

Mark Epstein
Mark Epstein Designs, Inc.
340 East 66 Street
New York, NY 10021
Page 1

Georgina Fairholme
New York, NY
Pages 22, 23

248

250

251

Photo Credits

Page 1: © Julio Piedra, courtesy Mark Epstein
2: © Dennis Krukowski
3: © Lizzie Himmel
10: © Bert Congdon, courtesy David O'Neill
12: © Viator Photo, courtesy Jane B. Viator
13: © Charles White Photo
14-15, 16: © Dennis Krukowski
17: © Phillip H. Ennis, courtesy F. J. Hakamian
18-19: © Phillip H. Ennis
20-21: © Bill Rothschild
22: © Phillip H. Ennis
24-25: © Peter Vitale, courtesy Mario Buatta
26, 27, 28-29: © Lizzie Himmel
30-31: © Lisa Masson Photography, courtesy Juan Pablo Molyneux
32, 33, 34-35: © Lynn Reynolds, courtesy Fox-Nahem Design
36: © Phillip H. Ennis
37: © Lizzie Himmel
38, 39: © Phillip H. Ennis
40: © Bill Rothschild
41: © Bill Rothschild
42, 42-43: © Dennis Krukowski
44, 45: © Paul Beswick, courtesy John Kraft and Susan Katz
46: © Dennis Krukowski
47: © Russell McMasters, courtesy Francis Gibbons
48: © Daniel Eifert, courtesy Katherine Stephens Associates
49: © Dennis Krukowski
50: © Phillip H. Ennis
51: © Lizzie Himmel
52, 53: © Peter Vitale, courtesy Mark Hampton, Inc.
54, 54-55: © Phillip H. Ennis
56, 57: © Dennis Krukowski
58, 59: © Phillip H. Ennis
60, 61: © John Vaughan, courtesy Gary Hutton
62, 63: © William Stites, courtesy Ginger Barber Design, Inc.
64: © Kenneth Rice, courtesy Agnes Bourne, ASID
65: © Agnes Bourne, courtesy Agnes Bourne, ASID
66: © William Lefevor, courtesy Daniel F. Burton
67: © Phillip H. Ennis
68, 69: © Sean M. Cassidy, courtesy Benn Theodore II, ASID, and Marie Johnston
70: © Bill Rothschild
71: © Charles White Photo
72, 73: © Mary Harty/Peter Derosa, courtesy Marshall R. Taylor Biddle
74: © John Vaughan, courtesy Leavitt/Weaver, Inc.
75: © Russell Abraham, courtesy Leavitt/Weaver, Inc.
76-79: © Dennis Krukowski
80: © John Vaughan, courtesy Joseph Horan, ASID

81: © Rob Super, courtesy Agnes Bourne, ASID
82-83: © Sean M. Cassidy, courtesy Paul J. Noël
84, 85: © William P. Steele, courtesy Harold Simmons
86, 87: © Lizzie Himmel
88, 89: © Barry Halkin Photography, courtesy Peterson, Weixler & Co.
90-93: © Langdon Clay, courtesy Robert K. Lewis
94: © Peter Vitale, courtesy Juan Pablo Molyneux
96: © Gordon Beale, courtesy Elwyn Colby Ferris and Marilyn Poling
97: © Creative Sources Photography, courtesy Oetgen Design, Inc.
98-99: © Bill Rothschild
100: © Dennis Krukowski
101: © Lizzie Himmel
102, 103: © Mark Ross, courtesy Gary P. Crain
104: © Phillip H. Ennis
106-107: © Eric Roth, courtesy Bierly-Drake Associates, Inc.
108, 109: © John Vaughan, courtesy Thomas Bartlett
110, 111: © Jon Elliott, courtesy Samuel Botero
112: © Phillip H. Ennis
114-115: © Bill Rothschild
116: © Phillip H. Ennis
117: © Bill Rothschild
118, 119: © Ferd Fromholz/ Photographic House, courtesy Florence Perchuk & Associates
120: © Derrick & Love, courtesy George Constant, Inc.
121: © John Vaughan, courtesy Parish-Hadley Associates
122-123: © John Vaughan, courtesy Agnes Bourne, ASID
124: © Bill Rothschild
125: © Dennis Stierer, courtesy Cheever House
126: © Phillip H. Ennis
127: © Mary Nichols, courtesy Roger Harned Interior Design
128, 129: © Russell Abraham, courtesy Dan Phipps & Associates
130: © Lizzie Himmel
131: © Charles White Photo
132-135: © Phillip H. Ennis
136-137: © Dennis Krukowski
138-141: © Peter Vitale, courtesy Juan Montoya
142-145: © Phillip H. Ennis
146, 147: © Dennis Krukowski
148: © Derrick & Love, courtesy Stephen Mallory Associates
149: © Lizzie Himmel
150, 151: © Phillip H. Ennis
152-153: © Dennis Krukowski
154, 155: © Peter Vitale, courtesy Marshall-Schule

156-157: © Daniel Eifert, courtesy Mayo-De Lucci Interiors
158, 159: © Phillip H. Ennis
160-161: © Hickey Robertson, courtesy Ann Weber, ASID
162-163: © Lisa Masson Photography, courtesy Piero Pinto
164: © Lizzie Himmel
165: © Michael L. Hill, courtesy Ronald Bricke & Associates
166-167: © John Vaughan, courtesy Paul Vincent Wiseman Interiors, Inc.
168-169: © John Vaughan, courtesy Joseph Horan, ASID
170: © Antoine Bootz, courtesy Parish-Hadley Associates
171: © Adam Bartos, courtesy Mark Hampton, Inc.
172: © Phillip H. Ennis
173: © Lizzie Himmel
174-175: © Jon Elliott, courtesy Suzie Frankfurt, Inc.
176-177: © Lizzie Himmel
178: © Boyce Graham, courtesy Glenn Greenstein
179: © John Hall, courtesy Stephanie Stokes
180-183: © John Vaughan, courtesy Joseph Horan, ASID
184, 185: © Dennis Krukowski
186: © Phillip H. Ennis
187, 189: © Joseph Mehling, courtesy Ivan Dolin & Deborah Habicht
190: © John Vaughan, courtesy Nan Rosenblatt
192-193: © Julie Ann Clayton Photographs, courtesy Peter Werner, Ltd.
194-195: © Lisa Masson Photography, courtesy Penne Poole Interior Design, Inc.
196: © Phillip H. Ennis
197: © Eric Roth, courtesy Benn Theodore II, ASID, and Marie Johnston
198: © Chris Whitney, courtesy Decor & Design by Camille
199: © Matt Prince, courtesy Hal and Melinda Kuehne
200, 201: © Creighton Higgins, courtesy Harford Community College
202: © Dennis Krukowski
203: © Eric Roth, courtesy Marie E. Johnston
204, 206: © David Richmond, courtesy Holden & Dupuy Interior Design
207: © Kim Sargent, courtesy Peter Werner
208: © Phillip H. Ennis
209: © Dennis Krukowski
210 (L): © Dennis Stierer, courtesy Ledgewood Interiors
210 (R): © Dennis Stierer, courtesy Jordan & Batal Interior Design

211: © Phillip H. Ennis
212: © Jack D. Neith, courtesy Patricia Crane, ASID
213: © Ted Hardin, courtesy R. Brooke Interiors
214, 215: © Phillip H. Ennis
217: © Kenneth Rice, courtesy Robert J. Fiegel and John Gypson
218, 219: © B. E. McCandless, courtesy Charles Damga
220, 221: © Phillip H. Ennis
222, 223: © Lizzie Himmel
224: © John Vaughan, courtesy Michael Taylor
226-227: © Billy Cunningham, courtesy Maureen Sullivan Stemberg Interiors
228: © Mark Ross, courtesy Gary P. Crain
229: © Balthazar Korab, courtesy Brian Killian & Company
230: © Phillip H. Ennis
231: © David Wakely, courtesy Edwin Turrell & Associates
232-233: © Charles White Photo
234: Dennis Krukowski
235: © Eric Roth, courtesy Adele Michelin Gross and Stella M. Mitsakos
236: © Dennis Krukowski
237-240: © Lizzie Himmel
241: © Dennis Krukowski
242-243: © Augie Salbosa Photography, courtesy Barbara Cleveland and Frances Y. Gassner

We have endeavored to obtain the necessary permission to reprint the photographs in this volume and to provide proper copyright acknowledgment. We welcome information on any oversight, which we will correct in subsequent printings.

252

Acknowledgments

A note of thanks

First and foremost to Kevin, Patrick, and Nicholas for their love and forbearance through it all,

To Roy Finamore, my editor, who understood my vision and made all things possible,

To Jean Simmers for suggesting the idea, and to Jean-Claude Suarès, Andy Stewart, and Leslie Stoker for encouraging the project,

To Sarah Longacre, Diana M. Jones, Jose Pouso, Brian Hotchkiss, and Marie Finamore for their help,

To John Sturman, my copy editor, for always making it sound better,

To Jeanne Casson duPont for her neverending enthusiasm and hard work, and especially for the Rigauds, Marlboros, and Diet Cokes,

To all of the photographers, with special thanks to Phillip Ennis, Lizzie Himmel, Dennis Krukowski, John Vaughan, Peter Vitale, and Chuck White,

And to the hundreds of people throughout the country who contributed in their many special ways to this project, especially Carole Aronson, Jane Borthwick, Mel Brown, Connie Buchner, Pat Casson, Ursula Clancy, Nancy Croft, Gwen Edelman, Sarah Eggleston, Patricia Fast, Karen Fisher, Fran Gassner, Jannie Gerrish, Delphine Gilly, Lynn Goldberg, Jena Hall, Neal Hanslik, Richard Harary, Kathy Harrison, June Hayes, Page Henry, Betty Joerger, Madja Kallab, Sarah Kaltman, Elke Kasman, Jean Lenhart, Nancy Lundstrom, Cody Madden, Janet Marks, Joanna McMahon, Diane Miller, Angel Morris, Kelly Mulvoy, Dianthe Nype, Margaret O'Neill, Charles Patteson, Luis Rey, Joan Routh, Rye Free Reading Room, Sam Schwartz, Madelle Semerjian, C. Ray Smith, Dennis Smith, Barbara Snedecker, Carolyn Sollis, Loren Swick, Kathy Tashjian, Arlene Travis, Betty Treanor, Donna Truglio, Paul Weaver, Pat Weigal, Daryl Weil, Judith Weinraub, Molly Williams, Ann Wood, Julie Wright, and Nancy Young.

Design
Diana M. Jones
Composed in Cochin and Century Expanded by
Arkotype Inc., New York, New York
Printed and bound by
Toppan Printing Company, Ltd.,
Tokyo, Japan